RUNNING ON EMPTY
The Life and Times of a Gas Station Attendant

BRANDON BOSWELL

RUNNING ON EMPTY
THE LIFE AND TIMES OF A GAS STATION ATTENDANT

iUniverse books may be ordered through booksellers or by contacting:

iUniverse
1663 Liberty Drive
Bloomington, IN 47403
www.iuniverse.com
1-800-Authors (1-800-288-4677)

ISBN: 978-1-4917-4264-8 (sc)
ISBN: 978-1-4917-4263-1 (e)

Library of Congress Control Number: 2014914474

Printed in the United States of America.

iUniverse rev. date: 08/19/2014

For Shelley,
Ashley & Tim,
Lindsey & Josh,
and Steph

CONTENTS

Chapter 1

Good Night, Sleep Tight, & Don't Let the Bunk Beds Bite

Growing older isn't always easy, especially when you find yourself faced with the horrible truth: I'm not as young as I used to be.

When someone reaches this conclusion for the first time, they'd better start bracing themselves for additional reminders that will now be coming at an alarming rate of frequency.

The realization that someone isn't as young as they used to be can sneak up from behind and strike without warning. It can occur when someone's birthday is coming up and they realize they're about to turn an age with a big fat zero at the end of it. They begin to experience a level of fear and uncertainty usually only felt by a televangelist during a tax audit.

This realization can occur while someone is looking through old high school yearbooks and suddenly realizes that many of the classmates they once knew as children are now grown up and married with children of their own. They now own their own homes and their favorite pastime is yelling at teenagers for running across their front lawn.

The realization that someone isn't as young as they used to be can occur when they have worked for the same company long enough to enroll in the company's 401(k) plan, which they eagerly do because they're only twenty years away from retirement and they feel they need to make up for lost time. They're also excited to learn they can purchase supplemental insurance through the company for only a few dollars a month and they can now rest easier knowing if they lose a finger during a freak accident at work with the pencil sharpener, they will get a $2,000 payout. Even better, if they lose the whole hand they'll get a $3,000 payout.

The realization that someone isn't as young as they used to be can occur when a person finds themselves asking odd questions they would never have asked just a few years ago like, *Of the two items, my life insurance policy and my bottle of hair growth formula, percentage wise, which one is currently providing me with the best overall coverage?*

This realization can also occur when walking through a parking lot past numerous Mustangs and Camaros and stopping in front of a sedan and saying, "Wow, I never realized just how stylish a Buick really is!"

Of course, let's not forget when it starts to become necessary to write down the dates of friends' birthdays and anniversaries in order to remember them, but those dates are still forgotten even after being written down. If you're a man with female friends, or a female wife, this can get scary because women really get angry when you forget important dates like their birthday, which is rather ironic seeing most women don't like to be reminded that they aren't as young as they used to be, either.

Of course, let's not forget that moment a person realizes they aren't as young as they used to be as they sit in the front of the television after a hard day of work, flipping through the channels with the remote control like it's an Olympic sport (if you're a man), and realizing there is absolutely nothing worth watching. For the first time in their life they say out loud, "Television was so much better when I was a kid." For me personally, that particular "not as young as I used to be moment" was the kiss of death.

⬛ ⬛ ⬛

Not long ago, I was having lunch with a friend from out of town and her husband who were visiting over the Thanksgiving holidays. They were a newly-married couple who, like me, are in their thirties. The wife and I have known each other since we were kids, but, since I wasn't able to attend their out of state wedding, it was the first time I had met her husband. I was nervous about meeting him and was hoping to make a good impression.

When they picked me up for lunch on Black Friday, they insisted I choose the restaurant. We ended up eating at one of my favorite places: a quiet restaurant near the Baptist church where the wife and I grew up and where I still attend here in my hometown of Jacksonville, North Carolina. It's not the flashiest restaurant in town, but every time I eat there the food is always great and not once have I had to suffer through a meal there while obnoxiously loud rock music is blasted over a speaker like in other restaurants where I've eaten. Instead, they played recorded instrumental music at a decent volume, which allows customers to communicate with one another from across the table without resorting to texting or sign language.

As we ate, we discussed many of the things people our age are supposed to discuss over a meal: our current jobs, our desire to have new jobs that have nothing to do with our current jobs, buying a house, starting a family, and other topics of discussion that honestly don't do much to aid the digestive system.

When you're single, relating to your friends can be hard once they get married, so it's important to find common ground and discuss topics that are relevant to all of your lives. Thankfully for all of us the common ground was how great TV shows were back when we were kids.

I personally believe television today stinks like an open can of sardines left out in the sun over a three day weekend. The crime dramas are too violent, there are way too many reality shows (I don't want to know how they do things back in the swamp, nor do I care what treasures are in a storage locker in Texas or any other state for that matter), and the concept of the family sitcom seems to have vanished.

Recently I was watching an old rerun of *The Andy Griffith Show*. It was the episode where Opie accidentally kills a mother bird with his slingshot and chooses to take responsibility for his actions by caring for her three baby birds until they can be released into the wild. It was truly a touching episode, and I don't know of any TV shows today that come even remotely close to doing such an endearing storyline, with maybe the exception of *Duck Dynasty*, one of the few great shows on today. Even if *Duck Dynasty* did a similar storyline, though, I believe the most likely scenario would be one of the grandkids accidentally killing the bird with a slingshot, and they take responsibility for their actions by being encouraged to tear the feathers off the bird so Miss Kay can cook it for Sunday dinner. I also have visions of Phil leading the family in grace as he thanks God for the improvement in his grandchild's hunting abilities.

As we continued to discuss our favorite TV shows while growing up, by the time the check had arrived, we had all reached the unanimous conclusion that *Rescue 911* and *Unsolved Mysteries* were two of the greatest TV shows made during our childhood. When I learned her husband had the same love for *Rescue 911* his wife and I had, I knew it was now permissible to include him in the "friend" category as well.

Most readers know exactly which shows I'm referring to, but just in case you're too young to remember, I'll provide a brief recap.

First, there was *Rescue 911*. This was a reality-drama series hosted by William Shatner that re-enacted true stories of ordinary people who faced dangerous situations and how by calling 911 they received the help they needed to survive their ordeals. They often showed stories of robberies, kidnappings, hostage situation, fires, and so on, and trust me when I say these stories were *very* realistic.

For me, the scarier the story, the more fun it was to watch.

The ones I remember best were the ones in which someone is home alone, a burglar breaks into their house, and the resident calls 911 while hiding under a bed to avoid being seen by the burglar. What I always found interesting about these stories was that it seemed to me that rarely, if ever, did the burglar ever look under the bed. This is sort of amazing when you consider that this show came out at a time when cell phones weren't as widely used as they are now. Instead, the person hiding under the bed usually had a house phone with a cord attached to it that was approximately one mile long. As they hid under the bed with the phone they had to pray they were being robbed by someone who was either totally blind or just too stupid to look under the bed and see that mile-long cord waving around like an unmanned jump rope. Maybe the burglar did look down and thought it was a skinny, venomous snake and didn't want to get too close. We may never know.

I'm sure that more than a few children had nightmares after watching *Rescue 911*, but it was so great to watch and taught its viewers valuable lessons, like the importance of dialing 911 in an emergency, or just as important, what *not* to do so you don't have to dial 911 at all.

For starters, I learned to never run with sharp objects like knives or scissors, always assume a gun is loaded, gasoline and matches can make for a bad combination, and of course, never try sliding down a laundry chute because you're just going to get stuck. Looking back, I may have also learned that last lesson by watching *America's Funniest Home Videos* as well.

Okay, so not every story on *Rescue 911* was a life or death emergency, but that's okay because if you wanted to watch something *really* scary, you always had our other favorite show, *Unsolved Mysteries.*

Unsolved Mysteries was an hour-long program that featured a variety of, well, unsolved mysteries. The only thing creepier than the opening theme music was the host himself, Robert Stack, who was one the greatest, if not one of the spookiest, narrators who ever lived. Many times he introduced a different mystery by standing alone in some spooky locale at night, and his deep voice helped put you in the right frame of mind to be scared half to death. If Robert Stack were still alive today, he would probably be doing commercials for those reverse mortgage programs you see all the time on TV, though he probably wouldn't last long doing this. Most people who would call for the informational booklets would probably be afraid Stack's voice would be the one they hear on the other end of the line.

For those of us who were avid viewers of *Unsolved Mysteries* as children, many of us would agree that the stories we watched on the show back then still haunt us today. It's been a while since I watched any reruns, but if memory serves, each story began with a scary musical score followed by a title in big bright letters that explained what the story was about like "ROBBERY," or "MISSING PERSONS" or "MURDER."

Even creepier than the stories themselves were the composite drawings of the suspected robbers and murderers who were shown at the end of the story. If you watched the show, you know exactly what I'm talking about, and you were probably as freaked out by these drawings as I was. Most of these suspects were not people you would find on the cover of *GQ* or *Cosmo*. If so, they could have had lucrative modeling careers and would never have had to resort to a life of crime. Instead, they looked like people who were turned down to be extras in a Stephen King movie because they were deemed "just a little too scary."

What made these freakishly scary composite drawings even scarier was when the camera came in for a close-up on the faces, and it looked like the faces were getting closer to you. This usually caused me to cover my eyes and move away from the TV. Maybe this was done for dramatic effect or maybe they just didn't want all the near-sighted viewers at home to feel left out, but either way I think we all could have done without seeing this.

▮ ▮ ▮

If you were to ask any regular viewer of *Unsolved Mysteries* which were their all-time favorite stories, most people would say it was the stories that fell under the heading of "THE UNEXPLAINED," also known as the ghost stories the show became famous for showing. While I don't believe in ghosts, I do, however, believe in spirits, both angelic and demonic. To me this makes these stories even scarier because as you watch them, it becomes clear from the start that the people in these stories were obviously not being haunted by the cast of *Touched by an Angel*.

Many of these stories followed the same basic formula:

1. Family moves into a house.

2. Family undergoes shocking paranormal activity while in the house.

3. Family regrets moving into the house and/or ends up fleeing the house.

Of all the stories on *Unsolved Mysteries* that used this formula, perhaps none were as scary as the story of the allegedly haunted bunk bed! I'm certain more than a few kids were freaked out by this one while they were growing up. It's been a while since I last saw this story on TV, and I can't find it posted on YouTube, so I'm relying on a combination of my memory and from information provided by the good folks online at the *Unsolved Mysteries* Wiki Page (http://unsolvedmysteries. wikia.com), so thanks, guys!

While I may have a few minor details wrong, here's how I remember the story: A young married couple and their children, who I think were portrayed by actors in this re-enactment, move into a house in a small town in Wisconsin. Near the beginning of the story, the real wife, whose face is hidden so you can't see what she looks like, is speaking about how the house they moved into was their dream house. It should be noted that anytime you watched an episode of *Unsolved Mysteries* and the person being interviewed was talking about moving into their dream house at the same time their face was hidden, it was usually a given the story would take a turn for the worse pretty quickly.

So, not long after this family moves into the house, they buy a used bunk bed for the kids to sleep in, and this is where this story gets really interesting. After the bunk bed is moved upstairs from the basement, very bizarre things allegedly begin occurring. For example, in the son's bedroom near the room with the bunk bed, the son claims his clock radio has begun changing stations on its own. Watching this story, it looked to me as if someone, or yeah, you know I'm gong to say it, *something* was controlling the dial. Needless to say, it appeared the kid was pretty frightened by this.

I'll admit that if I were listening to the radio and the station changed by itself, I'd be pretty frightened, too, unless it happened to be on Ryan Seacrest's radio show, in which case I'd personally be relieved the station was changed.

The story goes on to say that there were times when the children heard voices calling out to them and saw images of fire and an even an old woman in their bedrooms, possibly a witch. The family finally calls in a local pastor for assistance, but the paranormal activity continues. Finally, the father gets so enraged he calls out to the unseen entity, demanding it to show itself to him.

This proves to be a mistake.

Several weeks later, the father comes home from work early one morning, and as he's walking towards the house, he hears a voice in the wind telling him to "Come here." He follows the voice, which then turns into a game of cat and mouse for the next few moments, until finally he looks and sees that his garage is on fire. He runs into the house, sets his lunch pail on the floor, but then I guess he realizes, "Hey, my garage is on fire. I should probably do something about this." He returns outside, looks at the garage, and everything is fine, like there had never been any fire at all. He then goes back inside the house to pick up his lunch pail, which flies through the air and crashes back down.

If I had been the father in this story, I would have handled this situation a bit differently. When I came home from work and heard the voice in the wind beckoning me to "Come here," I would have immediately stopped right in my tracks and recalled everything my family and I had already been through. Then, once I determined where "here" is, I would immediately have begun running as fast as I could in the opposite direction.

Despite everything that has already happened, the family chooses to remain in the house! Later on, the father is lying on the floor of his children's bedroom next to the bunk bed because they are apparently having trouble sleeping (you think?), and fog appears on the floor and a voice calls to him saying, "You're dead."

Okay, now at what point would **you** have moved out of this house?

Again, the family calls the same pastor for help, and again, things don't seem to improve. Now, I'm not trying to attack the ability of this pastor, but it seems to me that whatever he did to try to help this family didn't do much good. If I remember, the pastor was from a Lutheran church. I'll admit I don't know much about Lutherans except for the fact they really like Martin Luther. I've also heard they drive Fords, at least according to Garrison Keillor. I'm approaching this story as a Baptist, though, and it seems to me if this was a Baptist family having to go through this ordeal, this situation would have played out much differently.

If I had been the father in this story, the minute I knew

beyond a shadow of a doubt there was an evil presence in my house, I would have called in the first hellfire-and-damnation Baptist preacher I could find and had him and the elders of the Baptist church pray in every room of that house for whatever was haunting the place to leave by calling on the name of Jesus Christ for help, which in my opinion would have solved the problem. After ridding the house of the unclean spirits, we would all have then celebrated by adjourning to the kitchen and partaking of a delicious chicken casserole lovingly prepared by the ladies in the church who serve on the official House Cleansing Committee, not to be confused with the House Cleaning Committee, which is separate from the Parsonage Cleaning Committee or the Church Cleaning Committee. (Every respectable Baptist Church is required to have at least 311 committees. It's the law.)

Let's fast forward to the end of the story. Not long after the garage incident, the father is working late again, and a relative is asked to stay with the kids and mother. (I wonder if they had to pay him to do this, and if so, how much?) The relative is lying on the floor in the kid's room next to the bunk bed and is eventually stunned by a figure which is never shown on screen, but regardless, he lets out a scream that could only be rivaled by Kramer on *Seinfeld* or the burglars in the *Home Alone* movies.

Finally, the family decides they've had enough. They pack up what belongings they can and flee the house, never to spend another night there. In the next scene, the bunk bed is shown being crushed by heavy machinery and its remains are lying in a landfill. I remember watching this and thinking, *Maybe if you guys had done this sooner, this all could have been avoided.*

The story concludes with Robert Stack coming back on screen (just in case we weren't already scared enough) to say the family moved and another family later moved into the home and reported no problems.

Whether the story of the allegedly haunted bunk bed is true or not, we may never know. If this family really did experience these events like they claim they did, I truly feel sorry for all of them, but I feel just as sorry for the family who moved into the house after them.

Think about it. You move into a new home, and out of the blue, you're contacted by someone from *Unsolved Mysteries* asking permission to film a segment in your home because the previous occupants may have been scared away by an evil presence. If I found myself in this situation, I would want to strangle my real estate agent. I wouldn't, though, because I'd be too afraid I'd still end up on the show in one of the "MURDER" segments where a composite drawing of me is shown that is so large I could be identified by my nose hairs.

⛽ ⛽ ⛽

As I was writing this chapter, I had this marvelous thought: What if the family with the allegedly haunted bunk bed had a burglar break into their house one night, and one of the kids was home alone and called 911 … and ended up hiding under the bunk bed! They could have made this segment a story for both *Unsolved Mysteries* and *Rescue 911,* and this could have been the greatest television crossover since *The Jetsons Meet the Flintstones.*

Here's how I picture it. *Rescue 911* comes on with William Shatner walking through some 911 communications center while all the dispatchers are completely oblivious to the fact Captain Kirk has beamed into the room. He says something along the lines of, "Tonight, true stories of bravery and heroism on (famous Shatner pause) '*Rescue 911*.' We begin in a small town in Wisconsin where a young child home alone receives the fright of his life (for probably the three hundredth time, but who's counting?). Actors have helped us re-enact these events, including an actor playing the part of the original 911 dispatcher who was unable to participate in this re-enactment because she is currently in therapy."

The screen goes black and quickly comes back to show a picture of the house late at night. The child is shown home alone, afraid and crying, which the kid was already doing even before the burglar broke into the house because of having to deal with that infernal bunk bed on a daily basis.

Regardless, the kid then hears the sound of glass shattering and runs into the bedroom to call 911 with one of those mile-long-cord phones. Here's how I imagine the actual 911 call would sound like:

> 911 Operator: "911: Do you have an emergency?"
> Kid: "Yes, I'm home alone, and someone just broke into my house."
> 911 Operator: "Okay, we have police in route. Where are you now?"
> Kid: "I'm in my bedroom. I can hear the burglar outside my room."

911 Operator: "Okay, you need to find somewhere safe to hide."

Kid: "Like where?"

911 Operator: "How about under your bed?"

Kid: (Hesitation) "My bunk bed?"

911 Operator: "That will work. Go hide under the bunk bed."

Kid: "I'd rather not hide under the bunk bed."

911 Operator: "Why? What's wrong with the bunk bed?"

Kid: "Are you sitting down?"

911 Operator: "Stop stalling and get under the bunk bed. You'll be safe."

Kid: (Yet more hesitation). "Well, we're going to have to agree to disagree on that, but if you say so, I'll do it."

(Sound of door slowly opening)

911 Operator: "Did I just hear a door opening?"

Kid: (Whispering) "Yes, the burglar just came into my room."

911 Operator: "Alright, stay under the bunk bed and stay calm."

Kid: "I really don't think that's going to possible."

911 Operator: "Well, try. You don't want the burglar to see you."

Kid: "I don't think he can see me with all the fog in my bedroom."

911 Operator: "What fog in your bedroom?"

Kid: "The fog that mysteriously appears since we bought this stupid bunk bed."

(More sounds in the background)

911 Operator: "I thought I heard someone say 'You're dead.' Did the burglar find you?"

Kid: "No, but I think the fog just found the burglar."

(Sound of screaming. Lots of screaming)

911 Operator: "What's happening now?"

Kid: "The burglar is running away!"

911 Operator: "Was he scared off by the fog?"

Kid: "No, I think he was scared off by the old lady."

911 Operator: "What old lady?"

Kid: "The old lady who shows up in my room and stares at me. She may be a witch. We're not really sure."

911 Operator: "Is the old lady still there?"

Kid: "No, she's gone, but she should be back soon enough if you want to wait for her."

(Yet more screaming)

911 Operator: "What's going on now? It sounds like someone shouting, 'Fire!'"

Kid: "It's the burglar. When he was running away from the fog and the old lady, he ran out of the house and saw the garage on fire!"

911 Operator: "Your garage is on fire?? Did someone set your garage on fire?"

Kid: "No, I think it's more like the garage set itself on fire."

911 Operator: "I'll dispatch the fire department."

Kid: "Don't bother. It's already put itself out."

911 Operator: "What do you mean?? Look, I don't know what's going on over there, but I'm dispatching the fire department, too!"

Kid: "Fine, whatever."

(Sound of police sirens in the background)

911 Operator: "I hear the police. Everything should be okay now."

Kid: (Sarcastically) "Yeah, that's what you think."

911 Operator: "Look, I think you're going to be okay. I'm going to hang up now. Do you need anything else?"

Kid: "Can I ask you a question?"

911 Operator: "Yes?"

Kid: "How'd 'ya like to buy a used bunk bed *really* cheap?"

911 Operator: (Sighing. Lots of sighing). "Goodbye, kid."

The next segment on the episode would likely be about the poor dispatcher who had a breakdown after taking this call and had to be talked down from the roof of the 911 call center.

***

It's been years since I saw the story of the allegedly haunted bunk bed on TV, and ever since I watched it, I'll admit any time I see a bunk bed I always get a little nervous. This story freaked me out so much after watching it I vowed never to watch it again.

Well, a few months later, after watching the story for a second time (I'm a glutton for punishment), I was invited to attend a Sunday school retreat at a Baptist conference center here in coastal North Carolina.

It was an overnight trip (yeah, I think we all know where this is headed), and as my friends from church and I walked into our cabin, the first and only thing I could see was the long row of old wooden bunk beds that awaited us. At this point I began to wonder if the back seat of the church van in which we rode there would perhaps be the best place to lay my head that night.

As the evening went on, we attended a worship service and had a late dinner. All throughout the service and the meal, I kept thinking about those bunk beds. I REALLY didn't want to sleep in one of them, but I also didn't want to share my fear of bunk beds with anyone else for fear of becoming the topic of the sermon that Sunday entitled "Why Brandon Needs Professional Help." Everyone there already knew about my unnatural fears of grapefruit and wiener dogs, and if they found out about my fear of bunk beds, they would now have enough material to do a three point sermon. (In the Baptist church, a sermon isn't official unless you have three points. That's also the law.)

I made a decision. As difficult as it was, I decided to face my fears and sleep in a bunk bed that night. I had to show courage in the face of adversity. With the number of bunk beds in that cabin, believe me, there was a lot of adversity.

Later that night, I finally crawled into one of the bunk beds. I can't say for sure why I chose the one I did. Maybe I thought that of all the bunk beds in the room, this one looked the least menacing.

Needless to say, it wasn't the greatest experience of my life. I can honestly say, though, at no point that night did I have any nightmares, though, basically because in order to have nightmares, you have to be asleep, which never happened. I just remained in the bed and stared up at the underside of the top bunk where whoever had slept there at some point in the past had been kind enough to draw such comforting images like tiny skeletons with messages above it that read, "You gonna die." I only hoped that whoever wrote this hadn't been blessed with the gift of prophecy.

I tried reassuring myself that I had nothing to worry about since the allegedly haunted bunk bed had already been destroyed years earlier. Even so, one question kept nagging at me: *I wonder if that other bunk bed had a brother?*

＊＊＊

Looking back on this experience, I'm reminded how fear can impact a person's life in so many negative ways. We're all afraid of something at some point. We may not be as young as we used to be, but fear can threaten us at any age. Its effects are like an illness that stops us dead in our tracks and cripples us if we allow it to do so.

How do you deal with fear in your own life? Do you hold on to it and remain living in its shadow, or face it head on by turning to God for help?

Our God, the Creator of the universe, is more powerful

than all our fears combined. Whether it's fear in our finances, our jobs, our relationships, or if you just don't like the way your bedroom furniture is looking at you, give all your fears over to God. Trust Him to get you through the dark times in your life, and let Him to carry you back into the light.

As we make our way into the next chapter, though, let me caution you. What you're about to read will be far scarier than any story about an allegedly haunted bunk bed. We'll be looking at one of the worst fears imaginable in a person's life, and how that fear became a reality in my own life: Spending the last four years working as a gas station attendant!!

AAUUGGGHHH!!!!

Chapter 2

I Started Out Pumped, but Now I'm Coasting on Fumes: A Day in the Life of a Gas Station Attendant

As mentioned previously, over the last four years I have worked as a gas station attendant. Again I say, "AAUUGGGHHH!!!"

I didn't grow up wanting to become a gas station attendant. It was never a childhood dream of mine. I wasn't determined to spend years of my life doing whatever it took to become a gas station attendant. If anything, I spent years of my life doing whatever it took <u>not</u> to become a gas station attendant. Unfortunately, because I was born with a vision impairment that left me legally blind, my employment options were limited despite all the years I spent in college and graduate school. Any job that required a driver's license was out of the question from the start, such as a police officer, firefighter, or a getaway driver for an I.R.S. field agent. Like a lot of guys, I thought it would be fun to have a career in sports, but being legally blind hurts your career prospects in the sports world as well, unless you want to become a water boy or referee. Plus, from what you just read in the previous chapter, you know I wouldn't work as a professional bunk bed tester even if the job was handed to me on a silver platter. When it came down to it, becoming a gas station attendant was the best option available to me at the time, and given the choice between this career path and unemployment, financial ruin, and eventual homelessness, I think I chose wisely.

The job of a gas station attendant is one most job seekers have tried to avoid, and popular culture hasn't done gas station attendants any favors in how they're depicted in movies and television.

Think about it. How many times have you ever watched a TV show or movie where a gas station attendant was held in high regard? You just don't see that very often. What you usually see is what many refer to as *It's a Wonderful Life* Syndrome where the lead character in a TV show or movie is going through a hard time and they receive a visit by a mysterious guardian angel who shows them what their life would be like if they had chosen another path. Usually, it's the "wrong" path, and on more than a few occasions, the character is shown ending up in what may be the worst possible fate imaginable by cultural standards. Yep, you guessed it: working as a gas station attendant.

I'm surprised Hollywood celebrities have not rallied to rid the world of gas station attendants. I have visions of actors doing public service announcements on TV saying, "If you or someone you know is a gas station attendant, you're not alone. There is help. Call your local Employment Security Commission for assistance."

For many years, I fell prey to this mentality myself, but after years of working in a gas station, things are different. Growing up, I watched scenes on TV depicting the daily life of a gas station attendant and thought, *Wow, this is the worst possible fate known to man!* Now when I see these same images I get excited and think, *Hey, I know what model of gas pump that guy's using! That's the Gas Pumpapalooza 2000! Not as good as the Gas Pumpapalooza 3000 model, but still, an excellent choice!*

As with any job, working as a gas station attendant has its advantages and disadvantages. Some disadvantages include working after dark and the annoying little fear of being robbed at gunpoint. Also, we aren't known for receiving large pay checks. I'm not going to tell you how much money I make in a year, but I will say that my ultimate goal is to make as much money per year as a public school teacher.

Another disadvantage is that many customers blame gas station attendants for the gas prices. Now, I can only speak for my station, but where I work, attendants don't set the prices. However, that doesn't stop some customers from acting like we've single-handedly ruined their life.

My theory is that customers see us just before they see the gas prices and they equate us with the prices. It's sort of like if you come down with a stomach virus right after eating a cheeseburger. The cheeseburger was perfectly edible, and eating it did nothing to make you sick, but you still got sick anyway. After that, you don't ever want to see a cheeseburger again because it reminds you of being sick. Apparently gas station attendants are like human cheeseburgers to some people. They see us and lose their appetites.

Another disadvantage about being a gas station attendant I'll discuss throughout this chapter is dealing with bad drivers. I've lost track of the number of times I've narrowly avoided being hit by a car. Thankfully, by the time the driver put the car into reverse and tried again, I had moved to a safer location.

Hey, I told you we get blamed for gas prices.

Seriously, though, there are also advantages to working as a gas station attendant. For one thing, I get to wear jeans and tennis shoes to work, so that's pretty cool. Plus, I can get in a workout on the treadmill before going to work, and I usually don't have to worry about taking a shower since gas station attendants are allowed to come to work with a slight odor. If we smelled good, our bosses might think we weren't doing our jobs.

Another advantage is that after years of watching customers drive into the station to fuel up in a variety of vehicles, I've pretty much memorized which side the gas tank is on for most specific makes and models of automobiles. Before a car pulls up to the pump and I even see the gas tank, I can know with 99.99% accuracy which side the tank is on, and I think that's a pretty remarkable gift. Why I'm still single remains a mystery.

🔋 🔋 🔋

During any given shift at work, a gas station attendant will answer a variety of questions from customers such as

"What time do you close?" or "Can I pay with cash?" or "Do you have a restroom?" Often times, we're asked these questions over and over, but we still gladly answer them, though sometimes we must fight the urge to get sarcastic in our responses.

Here's a tip: If you work in a gas station and someone asks, "Who supplies your gasoline?," never respond by saying, "It comes from Uncle Bob's Gas 'n Stuff. They're a local supplier. Their motto is 'If we've got gas, you've got gas.'" Here's another tip: If someone asks, "What is IN your gasoline?," never respond by saying, "It contains two main ingredients – ten percent or less ethanol mixed in with a little love."

Some questions I'm constantly asked really test my patience levels, though, with the one that takes first place being "What exactly do you do here all day?" This is usually followed by, "Do they really need you here at all?"

While neither of these questions has done anything to improve my overall self-esteem, they're still valid questions that deserve an answer. After all, the role of a gas station attendant has changed dramatically through the years since many gas stations are now self-service. This doesn't mean, however, that gas station attendants are a thing of the past or that we're not needed anymore. We still serve important roles and assist our customers in a variety of ways. Along the way, we also face many unique challenges.

So, for your reading pleasure, I will now share what a typical day as a gas station attendant has been for me over these past few years. After reading the following pages, it will become evident that God has given me the gift of writing not only comedy, but also the gift of writing drama, horror, and at times, science fiction.

The Background: Before I go any further, I should mention I'm not a typical gas station attendant. I actually work at an on-site gas station for a members-only warehouse club. If you don't know what a warehouse club is, it's basically a really big store where you pay an annual membership fee to shop there. You can often buy items in bulk, and it's been rumored you can purchase a jar of mayonnaise large enough to not only to feed a family of four, but when emptied, can also adequately house a family of four.

When I first came to work for "The Store," as I like to call it, I started out as a product demonstrator. I was one of those people who wore an apron, a hair net, and passed out free samples of items like granola bars and cream puffs or actually demonstrated products like a cleaning solution or a stapler. I don't like to brag, but the outcome of the day I sold staplers is still talked about today among my coworkers and will likely go down as one of the greatest moments in the history of retail, but that's just my opinion.

After working as a product demonstrator for just over a year, our department was outsourced to another company, so to stay within my company, I took a job in our Electronics department. I worked in Electronics for seven months, and many thought that was seven months too long. I wasn't as well-trained for the job as I could have been, but even if I had been better trained, I never really had a good grasp of it. Whenever a customer asked me a question I got really nervous and prayed it would to be one of the few questions I knew the answer to, or at the very least I could make something up on the spot that made the customer think I knew the answer. Sometimes I got lucky and was asked a simple question like, "What is the difference between 1080p and 720p?," and I could honestly say to the customer, "Why, 360p, of course," but rarely was I that fortunate. It was because of such ingenious responses on my part that everyone involved concluded a change was in order. When a position at our new on-site gas station finally opened up, I gladly made the move.

Little did I know...

Arriving at work: When I arrive at work, I don't go directly to the gas station. Instead, I walk into the main store and make my way to the break room upstairs to clock in for the day. When coming to work, I always wear a bright yellow reflective vest that is company-issued and required for me to wear while at the gas station so I'm less likely to get hit by a car. I also wear a bright-orange hunting cap and occasionally a bright-orange coat that are "mom" issued and required for me to wear for the same reasons.

As I'm walking through the store, I often say hello to numerous coworkers (many of whom are trying to hide the fact they are staring at my brightly colored work attire), and I make my way to the elevator to head upstairs to clock in for another fun-filled day of dealing with the general public. Our store elevator leaves much to be desired, and it has broken down on more than a few occasions. Because of this, I've always been a little nervous about the possibility of getting stuck in the elevator. The fact there are windows on the front and sides of it does nothing to reassure me. I have this fear of getting stuck halfway down and as I'm pounding on the door for help, the customers see me and begin laughing and pointing at me like I'm part of a carnival sideshow. The fact I'm wearing the bright yellow reflective vest, bright orange hunting cap, possibly the bright orange coat, and also I forgot to mention earlier my bright yellow gloves does nothing to help me blend into the background. If truth be told, I really do look like something you would find in a carnival sideshow.

Assuming I don't get stuck in the elevator, I make it upstairs and clock in for the day. After clocking in, I head back to the elevator to go downstairs. Going down the elevator is actually more fun than going up. For one thing, if I get stuck in the elevator at this time, I'm "on the clock," and I'll be getting paid while stuck in the elevator. Hey, if you're going to end up as the star attraction of a carnival sideshow, you might as well get paid for it.

Another reason I like coming down on the elevator is that children seem to notice me more when I'm coming down than when I'm going up. To see the looks on their faces as they watch me come down, you would think they were witnessing one of the greatest sights they have ever seen in their young lives.

They cry out, "Mommy, Daddy! Look what's coming down the elevator!" When they see what I'm wearing, they probably think I'm a cartoon mascot from a box of their favorite breakfast cereal, but still, they get excited to see me and the parents think it's cute. I smile and wave back because it's fun to be admired, if only for a moment. I know it won't be long until those kids are all grown up and blaming me for the gas prices just like their parents do now.

After leaving the main store, I make the short walk to the gas station. Along the way, I'm careful to avoid getting hit by any speeding cars in the parking lot so I can arrive safely at the gas station where I'll spend my shift trying to avoid getting hit by more speeding cars.

Our gas station has three rows of pumps under a large canopy where customers can fuel up from either side of the pump, which gives us the ability to have twelve vehicles fueling at the pumps at one time. Our station "headquarters" contains three small rooms. First, we have the main office which has large glass windows and a small desk that reaches from one side of the office to the other. Actually, it's not a desk per se, but rather a board held up by a pole, but it does have a desk-like feel to it. There is also a small file cabinet and a mini-fridge to hold bottled water. The other two rooms include a small restroom and an even smaller supply closet in the back. I love the supply closet because there are no windows in there, and in a pinch, it's a great place to hide from irate customers.

We also have a pay phone in front of the office. The pay phone fascinates the customers. They haven't seen one in so long they get nostalgic. I've seen customers just stop what they are doing and walk up to the pay phone and stare at it in awe. I can just imagine some older couple in an RV traveling through the area stopping to get gas, spotting the pay phone, and having this conversation:

> Wife: "Oh, honey, look! Is that what I think it is?"
>
> Husband: "Why yes! It's a ... pay phone!" I haven't seen one of these in years!"
>
> Wife: "Neither have I! Honey, get the camera! The grandchildren will never believe this!"
>
> Husband: "This has to be one of the greatest sights we've seen on our cross-country trip so far!"
>
> Wife: "I'll say! This pay phone is far more spectacular than any of those old covered bridges we saw in New England!"

After making my way through the crowds of the pay-phone paparazzi, I walk into our office to say hello to the opening attendant. Generally, I work the closing shift. We discuss what gas-station-related issues I need to be aware of, like broken pumps, gas spills, etc. Their final words to me as they leave help me determine how the rest of my shift will be like. If they say, "Enjoy the rest of your day," it usually means my shift will go pretty smoothly. If, however, they say "May the Lord in Heaven above preserve you with His mercy and protection," it usually means I should have called out sick.

Daily Duties: After the morning attendant and I say our good-byes (or offer our condolences, depending on how you look at it), I get right to work. Each shift has a checklist of duties for the attendant to complete before clocking out for the day. The morning attendant does such things as clean the gas pumps, check the hoses to make sure there are no flat spots or leaks, and clean out the underground fuel storage tanks next to the station of any excess gas or water.

I also clean the underground tanks, too, though it's not officially on my checklist. When I first began working at the station, I hated cleaning the tanks. If it rained hard at the beginning of the day and the morning attendant wasn't able to clean them out, it could take me a couple hours to get the water or gas out of the tanks. When cleaning the tanks, I constantly lean over to drop paper towels inside the tanks to soak up whatever needs soaking up and then remove the paper towels with a hand-held grabbing claw device. All the bending over has never done my lower back any favors.

In time, though, I'll admit I did begin to enjoy cleaning the tanks. If there happened to be a lot of water in them, as I moved the paper towels around inside the tank with "the grabber," I began to notice the sound of the water splashing around was rather relaxing. Sometimes I would even hear the sounds of sea gulls overhead since the gas station is rather close to the coast. At first, cleaning out the tanks felt like slave-labor, but if I closed my eyes while doing it, it actually started to feel like slave-labor at the beach, which made it more bearable.

My outlook on dealing with the customers also changed because of cleaning out the tanks. At first I didn't like being away from the main building at the gas station because it was harder for the customers to find me. In time, though, I realized that simple truth that anyone who has ever worked in the service industry comes to realize: If the customers can't see you, they can't yell at you. This realization has had a profound impact on my work ethic.

In addition to cleaning the tanks, I also have to maintain the trash cans at the gas station. At some point during each shift, I have to remove the trash from the large trash cans near the pumps and replace them with new bags. This is one job I have never grown to love. For one thing, the canopy I'm under acts like a wind tunnel, and when I'm changing out one trash bag for another one, sometimes as I'm holding the two bags, the wind picks up, and I have to keep both bags from flying away. I end up moving my arms in all directions and looking like one of those oversized blow-up dolls you see at the grand opening of a car dealership.

Another thing I don't like about emptying the trash cans is lifting the bags when they're full (and we're talking 50-to 60-gallon bags here). Sometimes the bags rip and trash falls all over the ground or worse, whatever is in the bag ends up in my face. Once I got sprayed in the face by some unidentifiable liquid from inside the bag that ended up going up my nose. I'm a germ freak, and this didn't sit well with me. Later that evening I called home to tell my mother what had happened, and she had to convince me that walking into oncoming traffic wasn't the best way to deal with the situation.

Another bad thing about emptying the trash is when customers throw trash in while I'm still leaning over the trash can replacing the bag. I don't know what *Dear Abby* has to say about this sort of behavior, but frankly, I think it's quite rude to do this at the same time I'm replacing the bag. It's even ruder when they throw the trash directly at my head so it bounces off my face into the trash can and they shout "Three pointer!", but that's all I'll say about that.

The Customers (Oh, the customers): A big part of my job is dealing with the customers who drive into the gas station on a daily basis, and I use the word "drive" rather loosely.

Let's talk about bad drivers for a moment. For years, men have somewhat playfully teased women for not being good drivers. After four years of observing both male and female drivers, I can honestly say that men and women are *equally* bad drivers. I have witnessed both sexes drive into the gas station in ways that have defied all logic and understanding. I can't say for sure what sense some of these people were born with, but I'm pretty sure it wasn't a sense of direction.

What do I mean by this? Well, the gas station where I work is designed to be a one-way gas station. The proper way to drive into it is to drive into the part where the word "ENTER" is painted in big white letters on the pavement. Then, after filling up at the pumps, you leave the station from the part where you see the word painted on the pavement in big white letters that reads (brace yourself) "EXIT."

We also have these things painted on the ground called "arrows" which are designed to show drivers which direction to travel to and from the station. Before working at the gas station, I used to believe every person old enough to drive a car had seen an arrow before, but now I'm not sure.

In my effort to help make the world a safer place (at least for me), I thought it would be helpful to have a quick review of Arrownomics 101. To begin, let me remind everyone what an arrow looks like. For your viewing pleasure, here is an arrow:

Now, when you see an arrow like this one, the pointy end is showing you to move to the left. Here is another example:

Now, when you see an arrow like this one, the pointy end is showing you to move to the right. There are also arrows where the pointy ends points up and down, but I don't know how to draw those on the computer, so let's skip ahead.

So, now that we're all on the same page, we can conclude that whichever direction you see the pointy end of an arrow pointing towards, that is the direction you should move towards, including at gas stations.

To make this concept even simpler to understand, I've devised a formula which we'll now look at in Arrownomics 102. For the proper way to drive into my gas station, here is the best formula:

FORWARD MOVING CAR + ENTER + → → + GAS PUMPS + → → + EXIT = SAFE AND HAPPY GAS STATION ATTENDANT

However, more than a few drivers who flunked Arrownomics 101 and never made it to Arrownomics 102 get this formula wrong. Instead they use the following formula:

FORWARD MOVING CAR + EXIT + ← ← + GAS
PUMPS + ← ← + ENTER = POTENTIALLY SOON
TO BE DEAD GAS STATION ATTENDANT
WHO NOW REGRETS NOT HAVING TOLD
HIS MOTHER HE LOVED HER WHEN HE
WENT OUT THE DOOR THAT AFTERNOON
ON WHAT COULD END UP BEING HIS LAST
DAY ON EARTH

When it comes to drivers not following the arrows and
driving into the gas station from the wrong direction, I've
heard a number of excuses from them. My personal favorite is
"I didn't see the arrows."

Now, we're not talking about dinky little arrows here. These
are good sized arrows, also painted bright white, and can be
seen from all over the gas station. The last time I counted, there
were twenty arrows. Regardless, many drivers claim they never
saw the arrows. IF this is true, perhaps these people shouldn't
be allowed to drive anymore. I'm legally blind and I don't drive,
and yet **I** can see the arrows. If I can't drive, but can still see the
arrows, why should they be allowed to drive if they can't see the
arrows? I wish I had the power to cut up their driver's licenses
on the spot and make the road a little safer for all of us.

My favorite excuse for drivers coming in the wrong way
is, "I'm in a hurry, and I didn't want to wait in line when there
was an empty pump in the other lane." This is when I must
fight the urge to respond, "Well, I didn't want to be a thirty-
three year old single man who can't drive, has no girlfriend,

and works part-time at a gas station, but that's the way life goes sometimes, now GET BACK IN LINE!!!"

Over the years, I've had more than a few scary moments with wrong-way drivers. Once I had an older gentleman drive into the station from the wrong direction at a higher rate of speed than I would have preferred, mainly because he was headed straight at me at the time. Despite waving my hands frantically to get him to stop, he continued heading towards me. Thankfully he stopped in time, but to all the drivers out there reading this, let me say this: When you're driving towards someone and that person is waving their hands and covering their face, this isn't the universal sign to put the pedal to the metal and aim for their head.

In my dealings with wrong way drivers, I have often been the victim of a "sneak attack." Many times, I'll be minding my own business, usually preoccupied with something like sweeping up absorbent from a gas spill, and suddenly, I'll look up and see bright headlights coming towards me in a direction headlights shouldn't be coming towards me. I now know what a deer feels like before its untimely death on a country road.

It really stinks to be a deer.

On one such occasion where I came close to being the topic of an obituary with the opening words, "Brandon Boswell, 33, affectionately known by his coworkers as 'Bambi,'" I managed to keep my cool and inform the driver that in the future they would need to enter the station from the right direction. Their apologetic response: "Well, you need to fix **your** arrows."

I love how some drivers turn the situation around so

even though *they* were the ones who came in from the wrong direction and almost killed me, it's still *my* fault they did this.

How can people have the nerve to make such stupid comments and think they can get away with it? That would be like if I retaliated against such a driver by jumping on the roof of their car and beating the front windshield in with a baseball bat, and later as I'm being handcuffed and placed in the backseat of a police car, I say, "This is *their* fault. If they had driven away faster when they saw me running towards their car with the bat, this never would have happened."

I'll conclude this portion of the chapter by sharing a story that came from a discussion at work with someone who wanted to know what could be done to make my job safer. I told them about all the times I came close to getting hit by cars, and their suggestion to keep me safe in traffic was for me to walk around holding a sign that reads, "Yield." I had to fight the urge to respond, "How about I go the extra mile and hold up a sign that reads:

"STOOOOOOOOOOOOOOOPPPPPPPPPP!!!!!!!!!!!!!!!!!!!!" 'Nuff said.

The Customers (Oh, the customers) – Part Deux: Now that I've shared my experiences with the customers as they enter the gas station, let's look at my experiences as they attempt to fill up their tanks.

Here's the process in a nutshell. Customers drive in (preferably from the right direction) and park at a gas pump. Next, they exit their vehicle and do the steps necessary at the pump to allow them to begin fueling. After they finish fueling, they get their receipt and drive away (again, preferably in the right direction). In theory this should be simple. However, "theory" and "reality" can be as different as left and right, night and day, or whatever comes out of a politician's mouth when they are or are not using a teleprompter. Some customers have literally shocked me in what they do at this point.

Let's start at the beginning. The customer drives into the gas station and parks at the gas pump. By now they should be exiting their vehicle, but instead, some just sit in their car for long periods of time and never get out.

Now, I'm not referring to drivers who have legitimate issues that cause them to need more time to exit their vehicle, such as someone with a bad leg who walks with a cane, and so on. A good gas-station attendant understands this and will do what they can to assist such drivers, including going "old school" and even pumping their gas for them if necessary.

I'm referring to the drivers who have the ability to get out of their car and fuel up in a timely manner. Instead, they remain in their car, completely monopolizing the gas pump as seconds turn into minutes and the drivers behind them gather in number and turn into an angry mob.

When I approach them to politely ask them to begin fueling, many times I look in their window to see what they're doing and I realize they shouldn't be doing it at this time. I begin to wonder if that same angry mob will let me become an honorary member.

I have reached the conclusion that gas stations should have rules posted at the gas pumps to instruct drivers as to what they should and shouldn't do when they pull up to the pumps. It should read:

ATTENTION DRIVERS: AT THIS TIME, <u>DO</u> EXIT YOUR VEHICLE AND BEGIN FUELING. IF YOU ARE UNABLE TO DO SO AT THIS TIME, PLEASE ASK AN ATTENDANT FOR ASSISTANCE. <u>DO NOT</u> REMAIN IN YOUR VEHICLE AND:

TALK ON YOUR CELL PHONE,

TEXT ON YOUR CELL PHONE,

TRY TO BUILD YOUR OWN CELL PHONE WITH SPARE PARTS YOU FOUND UNDER YOUR SEAT OR CONSOLE,

SMOKE A CIGARETTE, LEGAL OR OTHERWISE,

READ NEWSPAPERS, MAGAZINES, OR WRITE THE ROUGH DRAFT OF YOUR LAST WILL AND TESTAMENT,

APPLY MAKEUP TO EITHER YOURSELF OR YOUR PASSENGERS,

APPLY HAIR GROWTH FORMULA TO EITHER YOURSELF OR YOUR PASSENGERS AND WAIT TO SEE IF IT'S WORKING BY STARING AT EITHER YOUR HEAD OR THEIR HEAD WHILE HOLDING A STOP WATCH AND A PLASTIC RULER,

EAT A THREE COURSE MEAL,

COOK A THREE COURSE MEAL WITH NOTHING BUT YOUR CIGARETTE LIGHTER,

DISCIPLINE YOUR CHILDREN IN THE BACK SEAT OF YOUR VEHICLE, OR
GIVE BIRTH TO A CHILD IN THE BACK SEAT OF YOUR VEHICLE.

I realize that last one can't be helped sometimes, but childbirth can get very messy, and I have to clean up any mess made at the gas station. If possible, I would prefer to give the expectant mother directions to the next closest gas station so their attendants can share in the blessed miracle of birth, and better yet, they can clean up after the miracle.

So, at this point the customer should be ready to begin fueling. However, I still may have to intervene if they're doing something unsafe, like leaving their engine running or smoking a cigarette or allowing their five year old to fill up the tank. Most customers hate confrontation as much as I do, but I have a responsibility to try to keep the gas station safe for everyone, including them. Some customers can turn pretty mean when I tell them what they can't do. Sometimes they just stare at me and give me this really evil look and I can't figure out if they're possessed by the Devil or just suffering from severe constipation. I stand there wondering which would be better to ward them off, a crucifix or a container of Benefiber. On a few occasions, I was afraid the situation could turn violent. When faced with such situations, I try recalling what I learned from watching reruns of *Walker, Texas Ranger* and prayed if I ended up attempting such moves and kicked myself in the groin and fell to the ground that the customer would be laughing so hard they wouldn't notice I'd regained consciousness and crawled away.

Thankfully, so far, I've always been able to walk away from such moments. I'll admit, though, in my attempt to come off as Dirty Harry, I often ended up looking like, as one coworker so eloquently put it, "Barney Fife without the bullet."

I will say this, though. I've decided if I ever see a five year old kid smoking a cigarette while he's pumping gas, I'm going to just walk away because that's one kid who would challenge me to a fight and win.

Gas Pumpology 101: Okay, so NOW the customer can begin the fueling process. I say "begin the fueling process" because gas pumps today are so state-of-the-art it helps if you have a degree in computer engineering to know how to use them. At my gas station, the pumps are very high tech. Each one has a little screen where cues are given to the customer as to how to use the pump. They also display advertisements for items inside the store while the customer is fueling. Even better, if you know how to rewire the pumps, you can watch cable channels for free on the pumps. Okay, I'm kidding about that last one, but that would be pretty cool.

To use the gas pumps, first, the customer inserts their membership card (since it's a members-only warehouse club) into the pump by placing it inside a card reader with the black magnetic strip on the back of the card facing upward. Then, they remove this card and insert their payment card into the card reader, which will either be a credit or debit card, or one of two choices of gift cards, also with the card's magnetic strip facing upward. Then, they choose whether they want a receipt or not and are instructed to lift the nozzle. Finally, they select which grade of fuel they want by pressing a button, and then they can begin filling up the tank.

I think it was much easier to use a gas pump in days gone by. Judging from the experiences I've had with some customers I'm certain they agree.

Once, I had a customer, who, after I told them to insert their membership card into the pump with the black magnetic strip facing upward, it took seven attempts to get it right! When you consider there are only two ways to insert any card into the pump, either right side up or upside down, and it still takes them this many tries to get it right, it's pretty amazing. When they finally got it right, I bit my tongue and tried desperately not to say, "Congratulations! I didn't think it was statistically possible for you to make this many mistakes with so few choices available, but you proved me wrong, and for this, I applaud you!"

Gas Pumpology 102: Next comes the part in our fueling adventure where the customer begins pressing buttons on the gas pump. Personally I think this part is pretty simple. Customers are asked on the screen if they want to pay with "Credit" or "Debit" and they press the little black button next to the screen beside either "Credit" or "Debit." Then they are asked if they want a receipt and they press the little black button next to the screen beside either "Yes" or "No." It's all a matter of pressing a button, but of course, they have to press the right button. Even though the screen gives the customer guidelines on exactly which button to push, more than a few customers still need help. Even when I'm standing next to the pump and pointing right at the screen with my index finger straight at the button they need to push, sometimes they still end up pushing any button other than the one I just pointed at seconds ago, or in some cases, I'm still pointing at! For the longest time it amazed me how some customers never seemed to know which button to push, especially since the buttons are shaped like arrows.

Then one day it hit me. The buttons are SHAPED LIKE ARROWS!! Any customer who never passed Arrownomics 101 would have difficulty grasping this concept. Come to think of it, these were many of the same customers who drove into the station from the wrong direction from the start. Thankfully I can be a pretty good teacher when I need to be and the material needed to teach customers to pass Arrownomics 101 is the same material needed to pass Gas Pump Buttonnomics 101.

At this point, I usually walk away from the gas pump and let the customer do the rest. After all, at this point all they need to do is lift up the nozzle, select the fuel grade, and begin fueling. It's not difficult.

Sometimes, though, as I'm walking away, I hear that little voice in my head saying, "Brandon, turn around." I don't want to turn around, but I know if I don't there's bound to be trouble. When I do turn around, I'm likely to find the customer reaching for the Diesel nozzle when they should be reaching for either Unleaded or Premium. Even though each button is clearly marked with an "87" to press for Unleaded, a "93" to press for Premium, and the word "Diesel" to press for, well,

Diesel, they're still holding the wrong nozzle and are seconds away from potentially turning their vehicle into a $30,000 paperweight.

As I'm running towards the gas pump, I see the nozzle moving closer and closer to the tank as the theme music to *Jaws* begins playing in my head. By the time they have the nozzle in their tank and are about to begin fueling I'm now hearing the music from the shower scene of *Psycho*. Thankfully, I've always managed to get their attention in time, though sometimes it seems like I can't run fast enough or the words get stuck in my throat before I can get them out. Perhaps it's a good idea after all to walk around with a sign that reads "STOOOOOOOOO OOOOOPPPPPPPPPP!!!!!!!!!!!!!!!!!!!!"

Up From the Tank Came a' bubbling Crude: By now you're probably thinking, *Okay, they're finally fueling up. There won't be any more problems.* If you're thinking this, I'm afraid you're sadly mistaken. This can actually be the most dangerous part of the fueling process, especially if the customer isn't paying attention.

If a customer stays in their vehicle while they're filling up the tank, it increases the possibility of a gas spill occurring. If a spill does occur, by the time the unsuspecting customer realizes what's happened, there's a good chance the other customers have already run up to their car with empty gas cans because they think they've hit the mother load at the newly created "gas fountain."

When it's all over, I'm left with the job of cleaning the remnants of the mother load off of the concrete with a small broom, dust pan, and absorbent. The absorbent we use looks very similar to kitty litter, and if I don't get it up quickly, all the stray cats in the area will think they hit the mother load, too. I really don't want those cats dropping any "mother loads" where I'm standing.

Another way customers don't pay attention while they're fueling is when they run into someone they know and they start talking to them. They stop paying attention to the gas nozzle, and again, we have the possibility of more gas spills.

Do you recall in the last chapter how I talked about the different segments on *Unsolved Mysteries*? Do you remember the segments that featured people who had spent years of their lives searching for someone important to them? Sometimes at the end of the segment they would show footage of the two people reuniting. Usually someone would drive up in a car, and the two people who hadn't seen one another in years would embrace, laugh, cry, and so on. I believe there were occasionally cakes and balloons involved as well. It's pretty similar to those *Publisher's Clearing House* commercials. Anyway, to watch some of these customers "reunite" at the gas pumps, you would think they were being filmed by a camera crew for such a reunion.

Now, if some of these customers at the pumps hadn't seen one another for as long as some of the people on *Unsolved Mysteries*, I would be more tolerant and give them a little bit of time to get reacquainted, but this isn't the case. As I'm listening to these people talk, I realize it hasn't been years since they last saw one another. It's usually only a couple days or a week since they last had contact. Sometimes they still lived under the same roof but they just hadn't seen one another since that morning. Granted, it was early morning, but still.

When I have to break up the conversation, sometimes these customers get upset with me, but I have to do it to keep traffic flowing. What amazes me is that sometimes other customers who were pumping gas at the station at the time also get upset with me because I interrupted the customers who were having what they referred to as "a moment." The problem is, though, when they're having "a moment" at the pumps, the other customers directly behind them who are waiting to use the pumps have "a conniption" and get mad at me, and this increase the chances of my having "a coronary."

If this isn't bad enough, sometimes I've actually had customers leave their vehicles at the pump with the nozzle in the tank to fill up and just simply walk away from the gas station.

Once I had a man drive into the gas station in an RV. He drove the RV up to the gas pumps to fill up the tank, and in doing so, he blocked two pumps, which couldn't be helped, but it's still not the ideal situation. If this wasn't bad enough, though, he decided that instead of staying with the RV as he was filling up the tank, he would simply leave the nozzle in the tank and walk into the main store to shop! I didn't realize what he had done until he was already gone.

I suppose I should also mention there was a dog in the RV at the time! This is about as dangerous a situation as I've ever seen. I kept looking at that poor dog and wondering why any person would ever put an animal in such a dangerous situation. I kept thinking to myself, *Does he hate the dog? Did he just take out a large life insurance policy on the dog? Is he trying to make it look like the dog perished in a freak explosion?*

I stayed with the RV (and of course, the dog) to make sure nothing bad happened, and thankfully the driver soon came back, but to everyone reading this, let me just say this: People, if you love your pets, please don't do anything that might cause them to be barbequed alive! (Right now I'm tempted to do another *Duck Dynasty* joke, but I'll hold back.)

The End is Drawing Near (or so I think): So now we're to the point where the customers have filled up their tank, have gotten their receipt, and it's time for them to drive off into the sunset. Instead, however, more than a few customers choose to just sit in their vehicle (again). Are they stopping to reflect on the day's events? I don't know.

What I do know, however, is that yet another angry mob is beginning to form behind their cars. They're armed with car horns, and they're not afraid to use them.

When faced with this situation, the first thing I do is pray the customer at the gas pump will leave. If they don't, I'll have to confront them, and there are only so many Barney Fife impressions a guy can do in a day and maintain his dignity. When I pray a customer will move from a pump, it goes something like this:

"Dear Lord, PLEASE, PLEASE, PLEASE, PLEASE, PLEASE let that car move from the gas pump! OH, PLEASE, PLEASE, PLEASE, PLEASE, PLEASE let that car move from the gas pump!"

There are more lines in this prayer, but they're pretty much identical to the ones above.

Sometimes as I'm praying, the customer will drive away before I can even say "Amen." When this happens, the next words out of my mouth are usually, "Thanks, Lord! By the way, since you're listening, have you given any more thought about the chances of my getting a girlfriend before I die?"

If the customer still hasn't driven away from the pump by this point, though, I know I have no choice but to intervene. I've had more of these interventions than I care to think about. Sometimes I just want to walk out to their car with a set of pompoms and start cheering them to drive off by shouting things like "Come on, Honda, you can do it! Put a little power to it!" or "Go, Chevy, Go, Chevy, Go!" This actually isn't a bad idea when you realize that by now there's already a whole cheering section behind their car.

Again, I realize it sometimes takes some drivers longer to leave for reasons that are beyond their control, but all customers should remember what they were taught in kindergarten years ago about sharing and should drive their vehicles away in a timely manner so someone else can have a turn at the gas pump. (Gas pumps are like drinking fountains for adults.)

I really think some of these drivers have a death wish. Imagine a compact car just sitting at the gas pump while a dump truck is directly behind them with the driver blowing his horn repeatedly waiting to use the pump, and yet, the little car doesn't move. It's like watching a poodle taunting a cheetah. I must now do what I can to stop what can only be described a cross between a demolition derby and a *Mutual of Omaha's Wild Kingdom* special.

At this point, I walk up to the car and motion for the driver to roll down their window. I try never to touch a vehicle because I'm afraid if I tap on their window, they'll claim I cracked their glass and they'll sue for me for five hundred dollars in damages and a million dollars for pain and suffering.

When I do finally get their attention and they roll their window down, they often look at me like I'm bothering them. (Perhaps the text message I saw them sending at the time was really life or death and the fact they were laughing was their way of masking the pain.) Regardless, I remain professional and say, "Excuse me, but there is a large dump truck right behind you that needs to use this pump."

Does the driver say to me, "I'm sorry, I'll move right away."? Most of the time, no, because that would be the polite and logical thing to do, and with some drivers, politeness and logic are not part of their vocabulary. Instead their response is more along the lines of "@#*! you!" At this point they're usually now ready to drive off. (Well, at least now I know what words are in their vocabulary.)

I'm not going to conclude this section by telling you what "@#*! you!" stands for, but I will tell you that it's not *"Bless* you," that's for sure.

Breaks and Lunches: Let's be honest. When you were a kid, if someone asked you what your favorite part of the school day was, you probably shouted "Break time!" or "Lunch time!" As adults, though, if someone were to ask you what your favorite part of your workday is, you would probably shout, well, "Break time!" or "Lunch time!"

To most workers, breaks and lunches are more than just breaks and lunches; they are temporarily reprieves from the daily grind of their jobs.

Depending on how many hours I work in a shift, I take either one or two fifteen minute breaks while "on the clock." Since I stand for most of my shift, it's nice getting paid to sit down, if just for a few minutes. I also take a thirty minute lunch break, but I have to take this one "off the clock." This stinks because I believe food tastes better when you're getting paid to eat it.

When it's time for me to take any scheduled break, what I usually do is use my walkie-talkie to call for someone to relieve me at the gas station. At this point, usually one of our check-out supervisors (a.k.a. a C.O.S.) hears my despairing cries and arranges for someone to fill in for me. Often a C.O.S. can tell by the sound of my voice just how anxious I am to take a break, especially when I've been around heavy traffic during most of my shift. At work we even have a running joke:

> Q: What's the difference when Brandon calls a C.O.S. and when he calls an S.O.S.?
> A: There is none.

Despite their best efforts, it's not always easy for a C.O.S. to find someone to fill in for me. Usually the most likely candidates to become honorary gas station attendants are my coworkers from either the maintenance department or one of our "cart guys," the employees who make sure customers have shopping carts at their disposal and who help load items safely into customers' vehicles as needed.

While these days the people from both the maintenance department and the cart guys have good attitudes about filling in for me, there was a time not long ago when I preferred having a cart guy fill in because their overall attitudes seemed more positive than the maintenance people.

To be fair, when someone from either department fills in for me, they must take a break from what they were doing. I think this is why, though, the cart guys seemed happier to relieve me because their chances of getting hit by a car out in the parking lot where they work are likely much higher than at the gas station. The mentality of most cart guys has always seemed to be: *When Brandon gets a break, I get a break, too.* Those in Maintenance, however, at least during this period, seemed to have the mentality: *If I'm out at the gas station, chaos and pandemonium will occur inside the store, and I'll have to clean it up!*

At one time, a typical conversation with someone from Maintenance might have gone something like this:

> Me: "Hey, I really appreciate you coming out here!"
> Maintenance: "Well, you should appreciate it because by the time I get back inside, I'll be so far behind in my work I won't be able to finish what I need to do today!"
> Me: "Oh, I'm sorry. I'll get back out as soon as I can."
> Maintenance: "Well, I'm in hurry, so don't take one second longer than you absolutely have to!"

Me: "I'll do my best."

Maintenance: "Well, you need to be better than your best. I've seen your best, and your best isn't good enough."

Me: "I don't really know how it's possible for me to do better than my best."

Maintenance: "Well, knowing you as well as I do, I would have to agree."

Me: "Well, I'm sorry that years ago my father met my mother, they fell in love, got married, and I came into this world to grow up to be a gas station attendant at this store who had to take a fifteen minute break and needed your help."

Maintenance: "Well, I suppose you couldn't help being born."

Me: "No, that was totally out of my hands."

Maintenance: "Well, just don't let it happen again."

Me: "I'll do my best."

Maintenance: "Again, do better than your best."

Me: (Sighing) "Well, I'd better go inside now."

Maintenance: "Okay, try to enjoy your break. You seem really on edge lately."

While I've never had this exact conversation with anyone from maintenance, conversations like this aren't as exaggerated as I would like. I will say, though, I decided long ago that if I ever get married, I'm probably not going to invite any maintenance people to my wedding. I don't think I'd want them around my wife. It's for her own safety.

Cart guys, on the other hand, usually have a different mindset. For many of them, spending their workday walking around all over the parking lot is like wandering around in the desert as the Israelites did for forty years. When they work at the gas station, it's probably what it feels like to finally enter the Promised Land. At one time, a conversation with a cart guy might have gone something like this:

Me: "Hey, I really appreciate you coming out here!"

Cart guy: "No problem. Glad to help."

Me: "Listen, I may be longer than expected because I need to take the trash back to the compactor, too."

Cart guy: "No problem. Take all the time you need."

Me: "I should tell you that I need to stock up on supplies while I'm in the store, too."

Cart guy: "You do what you need to do."

Me: "By the way, I hate to tell you this, but I found out I have some computer work I need to take care of, too. It could mean an extra hour or so inside."

Cart guy: "Take an extra two hours if you need to."

Me: "I've heard the computers have been freezing up lately. That could keep me inside longer."

Cart guy: "No problem. You just make yourself comfortable and sit at that frozen computer until it's had enough time to thaw out."

Me: "Why, thank you."

Cart guy: "No, thank *you*."

Me: "Well, I guess I'd better run inside now."

Cart guy: "No, don't run. Walk. Walk slow."

Me: "You are aware that if I walk slow, take my trash back to the compactor, stock up on supplies, have lunch, take my last break, then do all my computer work, it's possible you'll be out at the gas station for the rest of the evening."

Cart guy: (Smiling) "Yes, I'm *very* aware of that."

Me: "Well, thanks again for all your help."

Cart guy: (Still smiling) "No problem. Enjoy your lunch, and don't worry. If, God forbid, while you're eating you choke on your sandwich and die, I'm available to take over your job at a moment's notice."

Me: (Nervous) "Thanks, that's good to know. Well, I'm going inside now."

Cart guy: "Okay, try to enjoy your break. You seem really on edge lately."

Again, I've never had that exact conversation with any cart guy, but a few have come close. I've also decided if I ever do get married, I don't think I'm going to invite any of the cart guys as well. I don't think I'd want them around my wife, either. It's for *their* own safety.

Atmospheric Conditional Surrender: As anyone who makes their living outdoors can tell you, working outside during the most extreme weather days can be rough. We often view the seven day forecast on the local news the same way Bible scholars view upcoming peace talks in the Middle East. These are the days where anything that can go wrong will do so, and this is certainly true for us gas station attendants.

The coldest days of the year can create many problems, and I'm talking C-O-L-D. I don't mean just a bit nippy, I'm talking colder-than-a-manager-during-a-yearly-performance-review cold. These are the days it seems the pumps malfunction the most, and usually at the same time the crankiest customers are using them.

I don't know which is worse, dealing with an angry customer outside when it's so cold I can see my breath or having to stand there while the same angry customer tells me my breath looks as bad as it smells. These are the days when I know it's only a matter of time until my morale and my body temperature will be in a contest to see which can drop the fastest.

For every second I'm forced to be outside, I can't be huddled in my little office with the heat on seventy-eight degrees. My only hope for staying warm at this point is to stand close to the customers as they're yelling at me so I can feel the steam coming out their ears.

Working outdoors during the hottest days of the year can be difficult, too. At least when it's cold, you can always dress in layers, but when it gets too hot, there are only so many articles of clothing a person can remove before the police are called out to investigate.

I've had to deal with some very frustrating situations at the gas station on the hottest days, too. For example, once during the middle of the summer as the temperature outside was climbing faster than the national debt, I had a motorist abandon his car at one of the gas pumps. The driver didn't bother to tell me they were leaving their car at the pump or why they were leaving it there. I just found the car, an Audi, parked at the pump with no one around. I kept waiting for the driver to show up, but no one ever came. I called inside the store over my walkie-talkie to have someone from Customer Service make a page over the store's public address system to have the driver come out to move the car, or at least tell me why they left it there to begin with, but no one ever showed up.

Perhaps it was the heat getting to me, but as I stood next to the abandoned Audi with sweat running down my face, waiting for a driver who never came, I decided to look at this situation as objectively as possible and I ask myself why anyone would want to abandon a car at a gas pump. And of course, the most logical conclusion I could come up with at the time was perhaps this was some sort of terrorist plot.

As I continued waiting by the car I considered putting my ear against the trunk to see if I could hear any ticking sounds that might be coming from an explosive device. Then I thought, *Hey, that's why we have managers, so that they can come out and stick their ears to trunks of strange cars to see if they can hear any ticking sounds that might be coming from an explosive device.*

Moments later, a manger walked over to the gas station and looked over the car to make sure there was nothing ticking, leaking, or oozing from any portion of the vehicle. He assured me it was unlikely someone would use an Audi to blow up a gas station. He actually thought the more likely choice of vehicle to be used to blow up a gas station would be a Ford. I'm not sure what he based that logic on; perhaps he drove a Pinto when he was younger. All I know is I've never looked at Fords the same way since.

(If what I wrote in the first chapter is correct and Lutherans do drive Fords, does that mean that scattered throughout

Minnesota and Wisconsin there are "sleeper cells" of radical Lutheran terrorists plotting to blow up gas stations using the family station wagon? If so, why would they want to do this? Did someone lace their tuna hot dishes or Lutefisk with mind-altering drugs? Who knows? All I know is that the next time Garrison Keillor goes on the radio to tell us what's been going on in Lake Wobegon, perhaps we would be wise to pay closer attention.)

Eventually, the police were called to investigate the abandoned car and soon determined everything was ok. I later spoke to a manager who, after talking to the police, found out that the driver of the abandoned car was someone they had dealt with in the past who allegedly had a history of mental health issues and was possibly off their medication and, not thinking clearly, just simply left the car at the gas pump. Later that day the car was finally moved.

Regardless, I wish "The Case of the Mysterious Potentially Exploding Audi" hadn't occurred on one of the hottest days of the year, but at least the Audi never blew up, because if it had, then it would have gotten much hotter.

I'll say this, though: If I ever see a Ford parked at the pumps with no one around, I'm going to get on my walkie-talkie as fast as I can and see if I can get one of the cart guys to quickly come over and do a break for me.

⛽ ⛽ ⛽

Perhaps the only thing worse than having to deal with customers during the hottest and coldest days of the year are dealing with them on the rainiest days right in the middle of a torrential downpour.

I think I can safely speak on behalf of most retail workers, regardless of whether they work indoors or outdoors, when I say that it's the wettest, nastiest, most miserably rainiest days that seem to attract the most shoppers. Why this phenomenon occurs is anybody's guess.

It never fails. It could be raining with wind gusts up to 70 miles per hour. Trees and power lines are down. Many roads are completely flooded. People are being rescued from the roofs of their cars by helicopters. Every politician within a hundred mile radius is on the way wearing their light blue shirts and khaki pants preparing for photo ops with flood victims. The forecast still calls for an additional twelve inches of rain by evening, and the police are warning everyone to stay off the roads. Most people are smart enough to heed the warning, but then there are those brave souls (and by "brave" I mean completely out of their minds) who think to themselves, *Hey, since there won't be much traffic today, this would be a perfect time to go shopping!* Because of this mentality, many of us retail workers feel a moral obligation to brave the elements to come into work so that our customers will still be able to purchase such necessities as gas, bread, milk, and scratch-off Lotto tickets.

For those who work indoors, these are the days when the roof will leak, pipes will burst, and you and your coworkers will be treated to the sight of a newly formed waterfall flowing from the top of the roof of the store straight down onto the most expensive displays of merchandise, such as flat screen televisions or diamond rings.

When this occurs, even the most laid back, happy-go-lucky manager has no since of humor. If you try to cheer them up by walking up to them and asking, "Hey, is it true the store has a new promotional campaign that if it rains IN the store on the day you get married, the engagement ring you bought in the jewelry department is free?" At this point the manager will politely smile and calmly instruct you to walk away before they find the first blunt object at their disposal and hit you repeatedly with it.

If you think it's bad working indoors during a rainstorm, imagine what I put up with outside at the gas station. Rain can bring out the worst in many drivers. On rainy days, it seems I deal with more impatient drivers than usual. They drive into the station from the wrong direction to avoid waiting in line or they stay in their vehicles to stay dry when they're filling up when they're supposed to stay outside the vehicle. Sometimes they don't need any gas at all but just drive under the canopy and block a row of gas pumps because they have multiple bags of toilet paper in the back of their truck already covered in plastic, but still, they feel they must protect their precious cargo.

These are all major concerns I deal with on rainy days, but there's one concern I have far scarier then dealing with the customers, and that's the fear of (gasp!) getting my socks wet!

I hate wet socks like God hates sin. If my hat gets wet, no problem. If my shirt or pants gets wet, so be it. Wet socks, however, are my kryptonite. The second one drop of water touches my socks I'm depleted of all energy and rendered totally helpless.

To avoid such a calamity, on the rainiest days, I try hiding out in my supply closet as much as possible so the customers won't see me and ask for help. This way my socks can remain dry the way nature intended it to be.

Somehow, though, the customers always know I'm there, and though they can't see me, it doesn't stop them from pressing the little call button on the pumps that I can still hear from my dry supply closet. Sometimes I think the customers can smell my fear. (Perhaps I should have showered that morning, after all.)

On more than a few occasions, I have tried to pretend that I didn't hear that call button so I can stay in hiding and preserve the dryness of my socks. Every time I do this, though, I hear the voice of the Lord saying, "Brandon, you have a job to do, and you need to do it." Immediately after hearing this, I hear the voice of the Devil saying, "Brandon, if you stay in hiding, sooner or later the customers will go away. Don't think about the customers, Brandon. Think about your socks! Right now they are SOOO dry and they feel SOOO good; all that will change if you walk out that door!" At this point the Lord counters by saying, "Brandon, you're a Christian, a man of God, with emphasis on the word *man*. Your socks will get a little wet, but you're feet won't drown and neither will you, now get out there and help the customers!"

After I come out of hiding, I'm wetter than I'd like to be, sock wise and otherwise, but I know I did the right thing, and the customers are usually grateful for my help, especially on such a rainy day. After they leave, I try to put the situation in its proper perspective. Sure, it's raining, and I'm wetter than I'd like to be, but God was right. I didn't drown.

On such days, I often recall the story of Noah and the great flood that covered the whole world. I remind myself how God gave the rainbow as a sign He would never again flood the whole world. Of course when you consider what Noah did to keep from getting his socks wet, you realize that hiding out in a supply closet doesn't seem so odd.

While the world has never succumbed to a flood while I was working, there was one occasion when part of the gas station was flooded, and the decision was made to close early and block off the flooded pumps. Unfortunately, to do this I had to walk into about a foot of water while pushing a shopping cart so that the person who was helping me at the time could take a roll of yellow tape and tie it around their shopping cart to block off pumps since our orange safety cones had become nothing more than floatable pool toys by this point.

As I walked into the water, I kept recalling countless TV news stories about children happily playing in flooded areas who ended up being attacked and eaten alive by creatures usually only seen on an episode of *River Monsters*. The fact that I can't see very well didn't help matters, and I had to assume that anything I saw floating in the water at that point may be alive with lots of teeth and had skipped lunch.

As I walked further into the water, I was thinking, *My socks are wet, my spirits are low, and if what I think is a tree limb floating towards me at this very moment turns out to be a venomous water moccasin, my last act on this planet will be to scream like a five year old girl, and I will do so unashamedly.*

As bad as this situation was, I reminded myself I still wasn't going to drown that day as once again I recalled God's sign of the rainbow. I did hope, however, that since my socks were as wet as they've ever been, that the next rainbow I did see had better have one major good-sized pot of gold waiting for me at the other end of it.

⛽ ⛽ ⛽

By now you might be wondering if there is anything worse than dealing with customers in the middle of a rainstorm. You bet there is, and that's dealing with customers in the middle of a snowstorm, of course!

I'll admit I love snow, but I love it the most when I'm at home watching it from my bedroom window as it steadily falls to the newly formed white earth as I sit in my recliner reading a good novel. Sometimes, though, I'm already at work when it starts snowing, and that's not much fun. I will say, though, that it is fun to see the looks on some of my coworkers' faces as the snow falls since it doesn't snow here in coastal North Carolina that often. As the snow begins to accumulate on some of the grassy surfaces near the parking lot, I'm certain some of my coworkers would love to go outside and build a snowman, but they realize it's unlikely our managers would let them do this unless perhaps they could sell the snowman a club membership.

What I don't like about working in the snow is dealing with the ice and sleet that often comes with it. The gas station is surrounded by concrete on all sides, and when it gets icy, it becomes unsafe for me to walk around there, especially since I can't always see where ice has formed.

If I'm scheduled to work on a day where there is already

snow and ice on the ground, I always try to call out of work because I don't want to risk slipping on the ice and hitting my head on the concrete. While I don't like to lose a day's pay and have less money in my bank account at the end of the month, I remind myself it's hard to maintain a lifestyle when you no longer have a life to maintain.

If, however, I'm already at work when the snow and ice begins to fall, I make plans to leave as soon as possible. As I'm walking back into the main building to clock out, I try keeping my balance on the pavement as ice is quickly forming underneath me. At this point I know I made the right decision by never pursuing a career as an Olympic figure skater, though I do believe a televised skating event called *Gas Station Attendants on Ice* would be entertaining, especially if Nancy Kerrigan would play the part of the gas attendant and Tonya Harding would play the part of an angry customer. I believe that would give it a sense of realism.

One interesting thing about working at a gas station during such days is watching drivers navigate through the ice and snow. I work in a transient military community and serve customers who grew up all over the country. After watching them drive in the snow and ice, I can place them in one of two categories: "Southern Drivers" and "Everyone Else."

As a proud lifelong Southerner, I don't want to put down my fellow Southerners, but frankly, "Everyone Else" in my opinion is far more fearless when it comes to driving in the snow and ice.

They've grown up in this type of environment. It's second nature to them. During their childhood years back in Minneapolis or Boston or New York City or Newark or wherever they were raised, their parents probably pushed them in baby strollers with little snow plows attached to the fronts of them. As they were learning to walk outdoors, they probably used little push toys that had little snow plows attached to them. By the time they were old enough to drive, their first vehicles were probably used snow plows. The money they made from using the snow plows to free their neighbors from their homes up North is likely how they were able to move out of the Arctic tundra and afford the beachfront property they now own here in the South.

Many "Southern Drivers" literally fear snow. Snow is not natural to them. My friends from up North can get a foot of snow and they don't give it a second thought. In parts of the South, though, if there is even a threat of getting an inch of snow, it's a prelude to the Apocalypse. We prepare for what could be our last days on Earth. We hold candlelight prayer vigils in our churches and pray for Divine intervention.

It's easy for me to tell the different between "Southern Drivers" and "Everyone Else" by how they drive into the gas station during a snowstorm, and by "snowstorm" I'm referring to that dreaded inch of snow I mentioned earlier. I don't have to look at any license plates to distinguish between the two types of drivers, either. When "Southern Drivers" pull in, they drive very slowly because they know that snow and ice are instruments of the Devil. They pull up to the pump and carefully get out of the car while wearing the heaviest snow suit and jumbo sized boots they could find. When they finish filling up their tank, just before they get back into their car, they make eye contact with me (their eyes are the only things still visible in their snowsuit), and from experience I know they want me to pray for them as they journey home braving the inch of snow.

"Everyone Else" is the opposite. They drive into the gas station at normal speed or faster, park at the pump, get out of their car, sometimes wearing shorts and a T-shirt and no coat because an inch of snow is like a heat wave to them. They fill up their tank and drive away like nothing is wrong. Some even speed away, as if being in the snow brought back memories of their time back in New York when they had to leave a gas station fast enough to make it to the East River in time to throw a body in before the surface froze over.

In short, "Everyone Else" thinks "Southern Drivers" are wimps when it comes to driving in the snow and ice. As a proud Southerner, though, I say we just know better than to attempt something so stupid from the start.

So, to "Everyone Else" out there speeding down the road laughing at us Southerners who hold prayer vigils at four in the afternoon because the forecast calls for a frost watch by nightfall and we need to get home, just remember that while you're poking fun at us, we're praying for your safety on the road as well as ours. When you make it home safely that night, please know our prayers for you were far louder than your laughter at us.

You're welcome.

The Prices, They Are a Changin': Other problems can arise at the gas pumps that are beyond the control of the gas station attendant. For example, at my gas station, gas prices are subject to change throughout the day. This is a sore issue for me because from what I've heard, the management is supposed to receive notification of price changes and then inform the gas attendants so we can make sure the prices get changed on the large signs posted at the entrance of our main store in a timely manner.

To date, this exact scenario has yet to occur, at least for me.

Instead, what usually occurs is the customers are at the pump filling up their tanks, and as I'm minding my own business, all of a sudden people are shouting at me from all directions saying, "Hey! What's going on here! The signs out front say unleaded is $3.20 a gallon, but this pump says it's $3.21! You're trying to rip me off!!"

At this point I must now rely on my former acting and improvisation training. Depending on the mood I'm in, a typical response to an angry customer might go a little something like this:

"I am SOOO terribly sorry! They're supposed to let me know inside when the price changes and they didn't do it! They NEVER do it! I can't believe they are putting me through this! I can't believe they are putting you through this! This is NOT acceptable! Don't worry, sir (or madam, whichever you may be), I will do everything I can to make this right! We value you as a customer and don't want to lose you! You just take your receipt inside to Customer Service and we'll do what we can to compensate you for your trouble! If you didn't ask for a receipt at the pump, I'll run into my office right now and write you out a receipt! If by chance I'm out of receipts, I'll find an axe to cut down the nearest tree so I can make some paper and then write you a receipt! Let me call ahead and let Customer Service know you're on your way so when they see you coming through the front door, they can ask the other customers in line to step aside so you can have first priority! Again, please accept my most sincere apology and know this whole situation has left me feeling like a poor excuse for a gas station attendant as well as a human being! I don't deserve to live, but if by chance God takes pity on me and allows me to go on, I promise on my life that I will never allow you to go through this terrible atrocity EVER again!"

Okay, I'm exaggerating a bit here, but no matter what I say, my goal is to catch the customers off guard so they end up saying, "Don't worry. It's not your fault. God bless you." My ultimate goal is to walk back to my office after it's all over and say to myself, *And the award for Outstanding Performance by a Gas Station Attendant in a Drama goes to...*

When Good Pumps Go Bad: Any long-time gas station attendant will tell you that after a while, the gas pumps they work around daily actually begin to feel like their own children.

It makes sense. Every day we look out for the well being of the gas pumps. We clean the pumps. When a pump runs out of receipt paper, we "feed" the pump more paper so it doesn't go hungry. We even "protect" the pumps from customers whose behavior may hurt the pumps.

I've come to believe that each gas pump even has its own unique personality. Some pumps are "the good pumps." They function well most of the time and make me proud to be a gas station attendant.

Then there are "the bad pumps." These pumps are most likely to cause problems like being more susceptible to a leaky nozzle or not working properly during a rainstorm and so on. These are the pumps that can quickly turn me from an "employee with a problem" to a "problem employee."

I'm most likely to discipline these pumps by walking up to the pump, pointing my finger at it, and exclaiming, "I've had enough of this unruly behavior, young pump! As long as you're living under my canopy, this behavior will NOT be tolerated!"

At this point in the pump disciplinary process, I place orange safety cones around the pump and bag the nozzle with an "Out of Service" bag to put it on a "Time Out" by leaving it there to think about what it did wrong. Then I storm into my office and reach for the phone to call the only people I know to call when a pump won't behave: Field Support. Calling Field Support is like taking a journey, specifically a journey I never wanted to take to begin with.

When calling Field Support, my first step is to get past what I call the "Gatekeeper," that annoying automated voice that always asks me to provide basic information like the last four digits of my social security number and the digits of my date of birth. (As many times as I've given my birth information, you would think by now I'd have received a birthday card, but I haven't.)

Next, the "Gatekeeper" asks what I'm calling about and I state my problem. I proceed to tell my problem by clearly speaking into the phone where I'm then given a message along the lines of, "I'm sorry. I couldn't understand you. Please speak clearly into the phone." I think, *I did speak clearly into the phone. You don't listen, that's your problem.*

Again, I tell the "Gatekeeper" what's wrong by speaking just as clearly into the phone, albeit much louder, but still the "Gatekeeper" responds by saying, "In order to help you, I must first know what you're calling about."

By now I'm starting to feel like the "Gatekeeper's" wife.

At this point the "Gatekeeper" tries to help me out by giving me suggestions as to what to say in order to get help, such as "You could say, 'Leaky roof,' or 'Broken printer.'" At this point I'm yelling into the phone and pronouncing every syllable of every word. Thankfully, once you shout, "B-R-O-K-E-N N-O-Z-Z-L-E! M-A-J-O-R G-A-S S-P-I-L-L! C-U-S-T-O-M-E-R-S S-C-R-E-A-M-I-N-G! F-I-R-E D-E-P-A-R-T-M-E-N-T I-N R-O-U-T-E!" the "Gatekeeper" usually cuts me a break.

Finally, the "Gatekeeper" "opens" the gate and let's me move to the next level, but I still don't get to talk to a live person. Instead, I'm subjected to the "Gatekeeper's" evil twin brother, the "Muzak Man," who protects the field support people by forcing the people who call them to listen to excruciatingly painful melodies for long periods of time designed to get on their nerves and cause them to hang up before an actual human being has to speak to them.

Usually I'm forced to listen to about five or six songs that were popular during medieval times, like around 1976 or so. I never hear songs with actual lyrics, but instead, I'm subjected to a series of tunes that others who have called Field Support in the past have described as a combination of xylophones and flatulence. While this isn't a particularly pleasant sound, it's still nicer than the sound of that horrid recorder I was forced to play in the third grade.

As I'm listening to these charming little melodies in my office, many times customers come up to me to let me know about other problems at the pumps, and I have to go out to assist them. I can't put down the phone, though, because if I do, the ten second period I'm away will be the time when the actual living breathing human being I've been trying to reach for the last forty minutes will come on the line, hear that no one is there, and hang up. This will lead me to start yet another journey with the "Gatekeeper," the "Muzak Man," and perhaps now their evil cousin, the "Soon-to-be-Dead Phone Battery."

When I take the phone out with me, I leave it on speaker phone so I can hear over the noise of the traffic. This is frustrating because I don't have the best phone to begin with, and if I turn it a certain way, I can't always hear what's happening on the other end of the line. As I walk around, I usually end up waving the phone around in the air to get a signal. Sometimes the customers hear the seventy's Muzak on the line, and when they see me moving around, they think I'm doing "The Hustle."

At some point in this ordeal, a human voice finally comes on the line and I no longer have to, as the old song by A Taste of Honey implies, *boogie oogie oogie* until I'm no longer able to do so. They say, "Thanks for calling Field Support. How can I help you today?" By now I'm fighting back the tears because I'm so relieved I got through, and someone is there to help me! Soon I'll tell them what's wrong, and they'll assign me a repair ticket number. I know some people don't like being treated like a number, but when I call Field Support, I'm not treated like *a* number; I'm treated like *multiple* numbers. Anybody can be # 5 or # 7, but how many people get to be # 4015678? At this moment I'm feelin' the love!

So, finally I tell them why I'm calling, and once I say what's wrong with the pump, they come back on the line and say, "I'm sorry, but that particular issue is handled by a third-party source. Let me transfer you."

Suddenly, I'm not feelin' the love anymore.

Soon I'm back talking to the "Gatekeeper," who, yet again, asks me why I'm calling. By now I realize a visit from the "Soon-to-be-Dead Phone Battery" might not be so bad after all.

Closing Time: Earlier I talked about some of the bad things that come from working outdoors, but there are good things, too, especially in the evening.

I'm talking specifically about sunsets. Until I started working the nightshift at the gas station, I never fully appreciated just how beautiful a sunset really is. How anyone can look at a sunset and a sky filled with shades of pink and orange and purple and still not believe in the existence of a Divine Creator is beyond my understanding.

There are many reasons why I love sunsets, but perhaps the greatest reason is that once the sun goes down, I know it's only a matter of time until my shift is over.

That doesn't mean, however, that after the sun sets I have nothing else to do. On the contrary, there are things I can only do at work at this time of day. For example, as part of my daily checklist, I make sure all the lights underneath and on the sides of the canopy are working properly. This is one of my favorite parts of the shift because as I'm walking around looking at the lights, I carry my clipboard with the checklist along with me. A clipboard is great to have around because when you carry it, people think you're much busier than you really are and usually leave you alone. Sometimes I'll stand in one place for a long time with the clipboard in front of me and just stare at it. It gives the impression I'm deep in thought and can't be disturbed.

After the sun goes down, the final hour of my shift is my favorite. I know it's only a matter of time before I'm turning out the lights, checking the restroom, putting the toilet seat in the down position (I work with two women, and I've been warned about my sense of direction, too), locking the doors, walking back to the main store to turn in my keys, and clocking out for the day. At 9:00 P.M, Monday thru Saturday and 7:00 P.M on Sundays, the gas pumps shut off automatically, so if a customer hasn't gotten their gas by then, it's too late.

Inside the main store, however, it's a different story. For most of the year, it closes at 8:30 P.M., but even after the closing announcement is made over the loud speaker, customers often ignore the announcement and keep shopping. Many times they continue to shop even after additional announcements are made that the store is closing.

I know this frustrates my coworkers inside the main store because they're just as tired as I am, and they want to get off the clock and go home, too. This is also frustrating for our night crew because they're ready to get to work but can't until the customers are no longer roaming through the aisles. They need the aisles clear so they can bring the forklifts out to restock shelves and occasionally break into spontaneous Broadway-style song and dance numbers. (Okay, I'm not sure about that last one, but I've heard stories.)

I realize it's unrealistic to expect all the customers to be at the checkouts within one minute of the closing announcement, but they should realize the employees have other things they need to do, and out of respect, they should leave the store in a timely manner. When it comes down to it, though, there's only so much that can be done to herd the customers up front to the registers with their purchases, especially since employees aren't allowed to use cattle prods on them.

Once it was suggested to get the customers to leave on time, an employee could chase them up front to the registers with a chainsaw while wearing a hockey mask to conceal their identity. This idea was ruled out, though, when everyone realized the chainsaw-wielding worker would likely be arrested and face jail time, even though they would also likely win Employee of the Month.

Another suggestion for getting the customers to leave on time came around Veteran's Day when the store was displaying a variety of older military vehicles and equipment. At the time we had an old rocket launcher parked out front, and that gave us some great ideas.

Imagine this: It's 8:30 P.M, and someone from Customer Service comes over the loud speaker and says, "Attention, members and guests, the store is now in the process of closing. At this time we ask that you make all final purchases and bring them to the registers located in the front of the store.

If you choose to ignore this request, please remember we are currently in possession of a rocket launcher in the parking lot that is pointed directly at your vehicles, and we will not hesitate to set it off at our discretion. The choice is yours."

This idea was also ruled out because of that pesky little fear of someone doing jail time because we weren't sure if the Department of Homeland Security would view this as an act of domestic terrorism, even though any person who did this would likely win Employee of the Year.

Again, though, I don't have to worry about customers sticking around, because once the screens on the gas pumps read that we're closed, my worries are over for another day. Soon I'll be clocked out for the evening and headed home. Depending on the day I've had, I'll either eat a little dinner and watch TV or just spend the rest of the evening at the computer sobbing uncontrollably as I'm updating my resume.

And that, friends, is a day in the life of a gas station attendant. Perhaps this is why internships at gas stations have never caught on with job seekers.

▪ ▪ ▪

As I'm writing this, I've been a gas station attendant for nearly four years. While it's not my goal to work at a gas station for the rest of my working life, jobs are hard to come by.

At one point, I tried finding a job back inside our main store but didn't have much success. I was given a binder by Personnel which contained a list of different positions inside the store, and it was suggested that I look it over while at work. While

I'll admit it was great having a binder to carry around to look busy (a binder is ten times better than any clipboard), I still found its contents rather discouraging. After reading over the various jobs and what they entail, I soon discovered I wouldn't be a good fit for most of them. Between my poor vision and my poor math skills, I wondered in which job, Forklift Driver or Accounting Lead, would I do the most damage.

Someone suggested I could try for a position in our store Deli, but I can't cook to save my life. If I did end up in the Deli or Bakery or Meat Department, it would be best to just go ahead and declare a public health emergency now to avoid the rush.

I'll admit looking at all these different jobs I wasn't really qualified to do had me pretty discouraged. I even looked at my current job to see if I was even qualified to do that. I'm not going to tell what I found out, but I will say that I did a very good job hiding the binder so my boss won't find out anything either.

🔋 🔋 🔋

Working at the gas station for so long has also affected my life in ways I never could have imagined. When I'm at home watching TV, whenever I see car commercials, I think to myself, *Yeah, that car is stylish, but how many miles per gallon does it get?* If I'm online and notice articles about current vehicle recalls, I read them so I can later inform customers who drive that particular vehicle about the recall.

Believe it or not, if you're a single guy like I am, this is a great way to meet women. When I see a woman drive into the station in a car that's been recalled, it gives me an excuse to walk up to her and start a conversation. My opening line is usually, "Excuse, me, but did you know the vehicle you're driving has been linked to over three hundred deaths due to faulty brakes?"

I'll admit this isn't the best pick-up line in the world, but it's still more original than "What's your sign?"

On long car trips, I find myself riding past gas stations and comparing their prices to the ones at gas stations in the last county I rode through to see which ones are cheaper. Also, when I see someone drive past with their gas tank open and their gas cap cover undone and dangling in the wind, I beg whoever is driving to speed up beside their car and blow the horn as loudly as possible to get their attention so I can make hand gestures alerting them to the undone cap cover. I view this as a public service to the motorists, though the Highway Patrol may have a different take on the matter.

I've worked at the gas station for so long now that when I'm in my office and trying to remember which pants pocket I put my pen in, I often say, "Now did I put it on the driver's side or the passenger's side?"

I guess I shouldn't complain, though. A friend of mine who works in our in-store pharmacy once told me that she's around so many medications at work that at night when she is trying to fall asleep she doesn't count sheep, she counts sleeping pills.

⛽ ⛽ ⛽

The Customers, Oh the Customers (The Revelation):

After four years of dealing with the general public, on more than a few occasions I've come close to my breaking point. If I manage to be polite, it's usually an act.

I once read a statement in our employee training manual that implied gas station attendants were viewed as ambassadors of our store. If that's true, during my next performance review, I'm claiming diplomatic immunity.

One evening at work, a woman drove into the gas station to fill up her tank. While she was there we began talking. She told me she ran her own store, and it became clear from the start she didn't have much faith in the human race. As we talked about our various experiences dealing with customers, I'll never forget what she said in regards to how she viewed the customers who came into her business: "Assume they're all bad."

It wasn't until this woman spoke those words that I began to play closer attention to what she was saying. The more I listened, the more she seemed like an unhappy person.

After she left, I continued to think about what she had said. I'll confess that after dealing with so many angry, irate, and downright mean customers myself for so long, there were times when I began to believe all my customers were bad, too, and this mindset made me a pretty unhappy person.

I decided this was as good a time as any to think back to the experiences I've had with some of my customers in the past. In doing so, I was quickly reminded of a very important truth:

They're <u>not</u> all bad.

In fact many, if not most, of the customers who have come into the gas station have been good and decent people. Many times they have thanked me for helping them. Sometimes they have even tried to show me how much they appreciated the job I do by offering me tips, such as candy. Sadly, company policy doesn't allow employees to accept gifts from customers. I'm not certain if lollipops and cough drops fit into that category, but I don't take chances where my job is concerned. Whenever I'm offered candy, I politely decline the offer. That's saying a lot, because I'm a Baptist, and we Baptists love getting gifts of candy or any type of food item for that matter. It makes us happy. In some companies giving candy as a gift is considered bribery, but in the Baptist church it's considered spiritual enrichment.

Candy isn't the only gift customers have tried to give me. Once at work I had a terrible allergy attack. At the time I was having difficulty breathing through my nose. On this day a young woman pulled into the gas station. She seemed nice so I struck up a conversation with her as she filled up. I mentioned my allergies were giving me a fit, and I would have given anything to have some nose spray to use right then.

After she drove away I put the conversation out of my mind, which wasn't hard to do since I felt so miserable. Later that day, however, this same young woman drove back to the station to give me a new bottle of unopened nose spray!

To say I was shocked was putting it mildly. Someone I had never met before that day had taken time to listen to my trivial complaints and out of the kindness of her heart had come back to bring me something she thought would make me feel better. Sadly, the same company policy about accepting gifts forced me to decline her kind offer as well. If I had accepted the nose spray and the management found out, I could have gotten into trouble. I suppose it's possible I could have even lost my job. To be honest, though, at the time I wanted to keep the nose spray more than I did my job. Not being able to breathe while working at a gas station, however, is far better than being able to breathe while standing in the unemployment line.

⛽ ⛽ ⛽

I'll never forget the time when, during an especially busy shift, I approached a gentleman who had driven into the station from the wrong direction, and I firmly told him he needed to move his vehicle. Needless to say, he was none too pleased at the prospect of doing this, but did so anyway.

Afterwards, I decided to walk back to my office. It has a nice sturdy lock on the door which has come in handy on more than a few occasions, and I figured this might be such an occasion. I stood there watching this gentleman pump his gas and was very anxious for him to finish filling his tank and drive away. Instead, after he finished fueling, he left his car and began walking in my direction. I felt confident he wasn't coming over to offer me any gifts of lollipops or bottles of nose spray. If either of these items were involved, I figured at best he would shove the lollipop up my nose or make me swallow the bottle of nose spray.

As he came closer, I began to ask myself the types of questions a person asks during these situations: *Why is this person walking towards me? Is he going to hit me? If he is going to hit me, how hard will he hit me? How many times will he hit me? When he's done hitting me, how soon will it take for an ambulance to get to the gas station? How long will it take the ambulance to get to the hospital? Will they put on the siren and let us run through red lights on the way to the hospital? Is there a chance that the person driving the ambulance is a lady paramedic who I once dated in high school, and if so, will she remember me? If she does remember me, will she keep the siren on and let us keep running through the red lights or turn it off and reduce the speed of the ambulance to less than five miles per hour?* (High school wasn't the high point in my life, and that's all I'm going to say.)

I was still trying to answer these questions when the man finally walked up to me. I took a deep breath and prepared for the worst. He took a deep breath and said, "Hey, I'm sorry." I had forgotten to exhale at this point so his words didn't register with me at the time.

Once I finally realized what he had said, I still couldn't believe it. I still had more questions like *Is this a trick to lull me into a false sense of security before hitting me?*

Instead of engaging in a fist fight, we ended up shaking hands. He apologized for how he had acted, and I accepted his apology. Later that day in the break room when I told my coworkers what had happened, they were as stunned as I had been. We thought this may be the first time in recorded history that a customer apologized to a store employee for how they treated them. When I told one coworker what had happened, she asked, "Did you look around for any hidden cameras?"

It's a valid question, but I knew I wasn't being secretly

filmed for any TV reality show. I don't believe any program currently on television would show a customer apologizing to a store employee. It's *too* unbelievable.

🔳 🔳 🔳

There are times when customers have reminded me how great it feels to go the extra mile to help others. Many times customers will drive into the gas station who were just there minutes earlier and ask me if I happened to find their gas cap which they realized they misplaced.

At this point I begin a one-man search to locate the missing gas cap at the gas station in the same way entire communities search for a missing child in a swamp. I scour the station from top to bottom, and if necessary, I search the surrounding parking lot in case the cap fell off their car roof or trunk. I feel it's my sworn duty not to rest until the missing gas cap has been returned safely to its rightful owner. I don't always find a gas cap when I search, but whenever I do I hold it up and exclaim, "Victory!"

When I walk back to the customer, I hold the gas cap out and ask, "Is this yours?" The looks on their faces are priceless, especially the female customers. To look at them, you would think I actually did find their missing child in a swamp. When I hand the cap back to them so they can see if it's the right one, they get excited as they're screwing the cap back into place. When they shout, "It fits!," it's like something out of a fairy tale. To look at them, you would think I was Prince Charming, they were Cinderella, and I had just handed them the glass slipper. I love this reaction, and I wouldn't want it any other way.

The male customers usually just mumble "Thank you" and drive off, and I wouldn't want that any other way, either.

I've had customers who taught me how a few kind words can turn a bad day around, and this is especially true during the holidays.

Now before I go any further, let me say for the record I love Christmas, but I HATE the Christmas season. Not only are many of my customers cold and cranky, but since it's flu season, some of them are also contagious. Some people debate whether to hang up banners that read "Merry Christmas" or "Happy Holidays," but I say let's hang one up that reads "Please Cover Your Mouth When You Cough." I also think instead of Santa Claus giving candy canes to the children, he should give flu shots.

Another thing I hate about the Christmas season is all the horrid "holiday" specials on TV. For one thing, most of them turn out to be these sappy romantic comedies set at Christmas, and all they do is remind me how incredibly single I am at the moment, and this makes me incredibly lonely. I think this is why I always make a point to watch the Charlie Brown television special every Christmas, because I can relate to him. Just like Charlie Brown, not only did I strike out with the little red-haired girl, but throughout my life, I struck out with the little blond-haired girl, the little black-haired girl, and also the little green-haired girl who turned out to have higher standards than I gave her credit for.

Let's get back to the Christmas season. I remember working during a particular shift last December when I wasn't in a particularly festive Christmas mood, thanks in part to some bad customers. It had been a long day, and all I wanted to do was avoid the customers for what little time I had left on the clock. I tried not to stand in one spot too long and risk getting seen and chewed out by anyone else. I kept walking around the gas station over and over. I seem to recall thinking if I walked around it enough times, it might tumble to the ground.

Hey, it worked for Joshua at the city of Jericho.

Finally, I decided to head back to my office. Just then a lady who was filling up her tank spotted me and said, "Excuse me. Do you work here?"

Immediately I thought, *Oh great. Here it comes. What trivial complaint does this person have that I'm going to have to listen to whether I want to or not?*

I put on the bravest face I could, but I was prepared for verbal battle. I said, "Yes, ma'am, I do work here. Is there a problem?"

The next words out of her mouth shocked me more than anything anyone could have said to me right then. She said, "There's no problem. I just wanted to wish you a Merry Christmas."

Unbeknownst to this lady, her words had turned a cold heart a little bit warmer that evening. Her simple act of kindness restored my Christmas spirit and reminded me the heart and soul of Christmas isn't found in a crowded store, but rather in a lowly manger with the birth of a baby who, through His life, death, and resurrection, would become the greatest "Must Have" Christmas gift the world has ever known.

* * *

Recently I had a discussion with a coworker about our jobs and our outlooks on what we do. When it came to my coworker's outlook on their job, they said, "It's all about the paycheck."

Since then, I've thought a lot about the outlook, "It's all about the paycheck." Maybe it's me, but it seems like the people with this mentality, regardless of how good they are at their jobs, seem the most unfulfilled.

Don't get me wrong. The paycheck is great, and if you want to keep earning them, you'd better keep doing a good job regardless of how you feel about it. With that being said, though, shouldn't a job still be more than "What's in it for me?"

When you work as a gas station attendant, it's easy to get discouraged. Every day customers drive into the station in expensive cars wearing expensive outfits going to far more exciting and better paying jobs than my own. Sadly some of these same people have reminded me in no uncertain terms they think they're better than me because they drive that expensive car or wear that expensive outfit or have that better-paying job. These are the customers who make me want to hide out in the relative safety of my office and never attempt to talk to anyone.

Here's the problem with this mindset, though. By hiding out

from all the bad people in this world, you miss out on meeting all the great people in this world. Contrary to the views held by many in the service industry, there are still great customers out there. I've met them, and the examples I've mentioned over the last few pages are just the tip of the iceberg.

These are the customers who take the time to learn my name and ask how I'm doing, which gives me the opportunity to learn their names and ask how they're doing. As we talk, if I notice they're having a bad day, I have a chance to cheer them up. I've learned that a few kind words, a compliment, maybe a good joke can make others feel better. When I can make others feel better, I feel better, too.

The conversations I have with some customers are far more than idle chit chat. Sometimes they get very personal with me. They tell me about concerns in their lives, and I listen to them. I promise to keep them and their families in my prayers, and many of them appreciate that someone is willing to pray for them.

Some customers pray for me, too. I know this because I was standing right there beside them at the pumps when they stopped what they were doing and prayed for me right on the spot after I told them about the struggles in my own life. These are the people that started out as just customers, but quickly became my friends.

Of course, it doesn't always work out this way, but it can if you're willing to make the effort. You may not have wanted to grow up to work in a gas station or a retail store or wherever you're currently working, but if that's what you ended up doing, make the most of the situation. Get to know your customers.

All the good customers God has allowed in your life will make you appreciate your job more, and all the bad customers will help you better realize how blessed you are to have all the good ones. In time your mindset will change from "It's all about the paycheck" to "It's NOT all about the paycheck."

Yes, I know some of you are reading this and smirking, and that's fine. In my next chapter, though, I'm going to share more experiences I've had in my working life, and I think you'll be quite touched by what you read. Even if you're not, just remember that if you bought this book directly from me, once I've "touched" the money you paid me for it, I'm not going to let you "touch" that money ever again, so you might as well keep reading.

Chapter 3

Milestones, Memories &
a Minivan or Two

This past fall marked a huge milestone in my career. It was five years ago last November that I began working at "The Store." As if making it to five years wasn't amazing enough, there was even a public recognition to add to the excitement.

I remember the occasion quite vividly. It was a few days after my five-year anniversary, and I was at work at the gas station. Early in the shift, I was on the phone with my manager who informed me he wanted to recognize my five year anniversary later that day at the evening employee meeting, and of course, I said I would be there. (Had I known sooner I could have sent out invitations.)

Several hours later I was inside the store for the meeting, which was held at a very exclusive location where not *everybody* is allowed to be. Actually, it was the back of the store near the receiving docks, but it's still an "Employee's Only" area, so that's still exclusive.

Soon the meeting began. The size of the crowd was overwhelming. There must have been nine, perhaps as may as ten people in attendance. The manager began the meeting by discussing store-related issues such as recent sales figures. At the time, though, I was only concerned that the figures would be sufficient enough to keep the store open long enough for me to accept my award.

Finally the big moment came, and it turned out there were two of us being honored that evening for five years of service. While I have nothing against my fellow five-year co-worker, I'll admit the wind was taken out of my sails when I found out I had to share the spotlight. In life, though, we all must learn to share. (Of course that didn't stop me from trying to find the brightest spot in the light and stand there before she could.)

Soon our names were called, and as we walked over to our manager to receive our awards, we received a standing ovation. Granted, we didn't have any chairs to begin with and had been standing up the whole time, but that still counts. The "award's package" was as follows:

1. A nicely framed Five Year Milestone Certificate in recognition of five years of dedication and loyalty to our company. (I remember thinking at the time this would be a great thing to put on my resume the next time I'm updating it after a really bad shift.)

2. A small silver (colored) five years service pin which came in a little box you first had to open to see it. (I think they do it this way to give the person opening it a sense of surprise. I remember when I first opened the box, I wondered if this is what it feels like for a woman when her long-time boyfriend proposes marriage to her and she opens the little box and sees the engagement ring for the first time. When I finally saw the pin inside, I'll admit I also wondered if this is what it feels like when that same woman finds out just how cheap her boyfriend really is.)

3. A Five Year Accident Free Certificate along with a Five Year Accident Free pin (I'll talk more about the pins later in the chapter.)

4. Last but not least, a new name badge for me to wear which read "5 Years of Dedicated Service." (I love this badge because the font used on it actually reads:

5 Years of Dedicated Service

I think it's great the 5 is so much bigger than the words because it shows up really well. Whenever I have to be in a rough part of town, I can wear my badge, and people can quickly see I've worked in retail for the last five years. At this point they'll know I won't have much money in my wallet, and I'm less likely to be mugged.)

After the awards were given out, my coworker and I made

a few brief remarks. I really can't remember what either of us said, but I know we both expressed our deep gratitude. If truth be told, though, my gratitude would have been a little deeper had the silver-colored service pin been a little less colored and a lot more silver.

❧ ❧ ❧

As I'm sitting at the computer typing the words you're now reading, I find myself glancing up on the wall next to me and looking at that five-year service award, along with a couple of plaques I was also awarded during this time period. None of this would have been possible, though, if the company hadn't taken a chance on hiring me all those years ago.

I've said it before, but it bears repeating that it can be incredibly difficult to find a good job, and that's especially true when you have a disability. I spent two years looking for work, and this was a difficult time in my life. Thankfully, by the grace of God, along with help of the North Carolina Division of Services for the Blind and a manager who took a chance on me, I finally found a job at "The Store." I'll always be grateful to everyone who helped me along the way.

Every award hanging on my wall represents a specific milestone in my career, but it's the experiences I've had along the way that have given me some of the greatest memories in my life and helped to make me into who I am today.

The stories you will read in the following pages are accounts of my fondest moments of working at and for "The Store." Not every story is about an experience where I received an award that now hangs on my wall, but these experiences forever remain in my heart.

◙ ◙ ◙

"Perspectives on Inclusion": Let's talk about traveling for a moment. For me, talking about traveling is usually more enjoyable than doing it.

I have always been a homebody. I like being at home. It's at home where my nice recliner and nice television are located. When I'm not at work at the gas station, I'm usually at home sitting in my nice recliner and watching my nice television, usually tuned to either a police show or the local TV news, listening to stories about escaped convicts who are traveling around robbing local gas stations and shooting gas station attendants. It's at these moments I find it to be the ideal time to schedule my annual paid vacation. Once on vacation, I remain at home in my nice recliner watching my nice television while not getting shot by escaped convicts (and getting paid not to get shot, too, I might add.)

As much as I dislike traveling, however, I've also learned when an opportunity comes along to do something great, sometimes you have to be willing to get out of your comfort zone.

Case in point, a few years ago my company celebrated the twentieth anniversary of the passing of the Americans with Disabilities Act (ADA). In the months leading up to this event, I had spoken at our store's annual disability awareness event about living and working with a disability. It was a great experience, but nothing seemed to come from it, so I just put it out of my mind.

Months later, however, my store manager at the time informed me that as part of the celebration of the passing of the ADA, the company wanted to recognize me for my service. He went on to tell me we had been invited by Home Office to fly out to San Francisco the following month to learn about events that occurred there that were forerunners to the eventual passing of the ADA. While in San Francisco, we would also have the opportunity to visit organizations that were helping persons with disabilities in the Bay Area.

As much as I dislike traveling, I'll admit I always wanted to see what California was like, and I knew this might be my only chance. (When you live in the South, you hear lots of stories about life in California, and sometimes they're even good ones.) I also knew that taking this trip could be great in helping me deal with my fear of flying. My view at the time was "If I never fly in a plane, then I'm likely to never crash in one."

Despite all my fears, I said yes to my manager. I knew I couldn't pass up this opportunity. Besides, at the time I was working in Electronics and I stunk at my job. I figured for every day Home Office wanted me out on the West Coast, that's one fewer day I would have to worry about doing something stupid at work and getting fired here on the East Coast.

I couldn't wait to get home that evening so I could tell my mother the news that in a few weeks I would be flying to California, and how this trip would be great in helping me face my fears about flying. Of course, once I told her all this, we then had to deal with *her* fears about me flying. At the time my mother and I were the only ones in our family who had never flown, and to date, she still hasn't flown and has no desire to. She says that the first time she flies will be when Jesus returns and she's taken up in the Rapture.

In the weeks leading up to the trip, things began to fall into place. By now I learned that in addition to my manager making the cross-country flight with me, my good friend Kim, who was my counselor with NC Division of Services for the Blind at the time, had also been invited and happily agreed to go.

The day of the trip finally arrived. My packing was finally done (by my mother, who didn't trust me to do it myself). She made certain every article of clothing and every toiletry was in its proper place and that every bottle that contained any form of liquid was small enough so I wouldn't violate any FAA regulations. When it comes down to it, my mother is a one-woman Department of Homeland Security.

Soon it was time to head to the airport to meet Kim and my manager for the flight. An hour later, we arrived at the regional airport in Wilmington. The check-in went fine, and I soon handed over my one piece of luggage to the airline officials for safekeeping. Thankfully the company was paying for most of our expenses for this trip, which was a relief since the fee to carry on the one piece of luggage could have easily bankrupted me. A few minutes later, we all said our good-byes, held hands, and prayed for a safe trip.

Soon, my parents were out of sight, and my manager, Kim, and I were on our way to undergo the mandatory security procedures before boarding the plane. We removed our shoes, belts, and any items in our pockets and placed them in small plastic containers to be x-rayed. Then we walked through the metal detector, and within moments, we were reunited with our possessions on "the other side." After a few more minutes, we boarded the plane for a commuter flight to Charlotte, where we would then board the plane to San Francisco.

I won't spend a lot of time discussing our flights, because, honestly, there really isn't much to discuss. From start to finish, it all went pretty smoothly. (Sometimes the best gift God can give a writer who's a nervous flyer is a lack of material to write about.) There are a few highlights and pointers about flying I will share, though.

First, when flying, it's always great to travel with a friend, in this case my friend Kim, since my manager was assigned to another row of seats and we couldn't sit together. Not only does traveling with a friend give you someone to talk with during the flight, but if you beg them enough, they might be willing to switch seats with you so you can have the aisle seat and they can sit in the center next to the person you weren't wild about sitting next to anyway who spent most of the flight staring at the back of the head of the person in front of them and nervously eating small finger foods which made them look like a squirrel who got a hold of some "bad" nuts.

Also, when traveling, especially cross-country, you will want to bring plenty of reading material along in case your friend decides to sleep on the plane or pretends to be asleep so they don't have to talk to you. I know many people are now hooked on these little electronic gadgets that can read the book for them so they don't have to, but I still like to have an actual book in my hand. In my case, I brought along a hardcover novel that was over 250 pages long that I vowed to read from cover to cover during the flight, along with a couple of car magazines I planned to casually glance at once in a while. By the end of the flight I had made it to page 19 in the novel and had read the car magazines from cover to cover. I have no regrets.

Another thing about flying I want to mention is using extreme caution when using an airplane bathroom. Not only are there health issues you need to be aware of when using these facilities, but you must also be careful not to use them while the plane is undergoing turbulence. In order to maintain your equilibrium, you must undergo a balancing act only a trained circus performer could pull off.

After landing in San Francisco, my manager, Kim, and I made our way through the airport terminal, picked up our luggage, met our driver, and soon we were being driven from the airport to Fisherman's Wharf for dinner.

As we drove away from the airport, I kept looking out the van window for my first glimpse of the sights of San Francisco. As I wrote earlier, when you grow up in the South, you hear lots of stories about life in California, especially San Francisco. I anticipated my first images of the city would be streets filled with radical long-haired protesters that looked like they placed first in either a Charles Manson or Lady Gaga look-alike contest. I also thought they would be waving signs protesting the unfair treatment of tofu and driving around in old Volkswagen vans with peace signs painted all over or perhaps a Toyota Prius with a gun rack on top.

Well, the gun-toting, Prius-driving hippies must have been in hiding, because at no point in our ride to dinner did I never see anyone like this, though I'll admit there were a lot of Priuses roaming around the vicinity.

After dinner (which I'll talk about momentarily), we were driven to our hotel located downtown in the Financial District. Along the way we saw the sights and sounds of downtown San Francisco after dark. I don't want to sound judgmental, but for those people back home with shocking stories about life in San Francisco, I'm pretty sure they had ridden through downtown San Francisco after dark themselves. While I can't recall everything I saw, on at least three occasions I thought I spotted Lady Gaga driving a Prius with a gun rack on top.

A few minutes later, we arrived at our hotel. We checked in and headed up the elevator to our rooms. As I walked into my room, the first thing I saw was the view of the city from the window. If you've never seen the lights of downtown San Francisco after dark from twenty stories up, you've missed out on something amazing. As I looked out the window, I wasn't sure what would happen over the remainder of the trip, but one thing was for sure; we definitely weren't in Eastern North Carolina anymore.

🞂 🞂 🞂

The following pages in this section focus on the highlights of my time in San Francisco. I hope that what you read will be a blessing to you just as the experiences I wrote about were a blessing to me. (Note: The Web addresses for the following organizations are also the source of much of the information I've included in these pages.)

Let's start at the beginning. The trip to San Francisco went by the official title, "Perspectives on Inclusion." While I already mentioned the trip was to highlight events from the Bay Area which helped to pave the way for the later passing of the Americans with Disabilities Act in 1990, this trip also became much more to me and everyone else fortunate enough to attend.

The purpose of this trip was to not only gain a better understanding of the early days of the movements of Americans with disabilities, but also help us gain a better understanding of how to better interact with people with disabilities, both professionally and personally.

I'll begin by going back and sharing the details of our dinner that first evening at Fisherman's Wharf. When my manager, Kim, and I arrived we were introduced to a variety of individuals ranging from officials from Home Office to other store employees within our company. While we all had different backgrounds, one thing we all had in common was that either we or someone we were close to was impacted by a disability. We even had a film crew along to document our experiences.

Since we arrived later than everyone else, Kim and my manager were seated at remaining seats on one end of the table and I was seated at the other end. When you work part-time in a retail store and you find yourself getting invited to dine with the folks from Home Office three thousand miles away from home, it can be scary, especially when there is a film crew on hand. As they filmed us, I prayed I wouldn't end up so nervous that I tried cutting my steak with my index fingers.

Our guest speaker that evening was Robert David Hall, the actor who has played the role of Dr. Robbins on the television series, *CSI: Crime Scene Investigation*. Tragically, Mr. Hall was seriously injured in an automobile accident years earlier, and as a result, his legs were amputated and he must now use prosthetic limbs. If any person had the right to be bitter, it would be Robert David Hall. Instead, he chose not to allow his disability to keep him from living his life. He spoke of how his disability created unique opportunities for him as an actor. Throughout his career, he has played roles on both television and in the movies that have encouraged and inspired others. As Mr. Hall spoke, I was reminded of the importance of not focusing on the things someone with a disability can't do, but rather, focus on all the things they can still do despite their disability.

The following morning, we boarded our vans to travel to nearby Berkeley, California, a city with a truly unique background. You can feel a certain indescribable energy while in Berkeley, and regardless of where you stand politically, when you're there you just have this incredible urge to protest something. It doesn't matter what. As long as you get to carry around a picket sign with a circle with a line through the middle of it, you're all set. The official motto of Berkeley could very well be "Heck, No. We Won't Go!"

After breakfast at a local café and a brief walking tour of

the campus of UC-Berkeley, we headed over to the Center for Independent Living (CIL) (www.cilberkeley.org.). This organization was created by persons with disabilities and provides programs with a wide variety of services which meet the needs of people with disabilities in their community. These services include such things as independent living skills training, peer counseling, and assistive technology training. The CIL has served as a model of hundreds of independent living centers throughout the U.S. as well as other countries.

While our visit to the CIL had many interesting moments, what I remember most was a discussion about the right and wrong ways to interact with and view the disabled. We discussed the use of the phrases "disabled person" versus "person with a disability." We were told that the proper phrase to use was "person with a disability."

When I first heard this I was rolling my eyes and thinking, *Here we go. Someone from Berkeley preaching to the rest of us about being politically correct.* My mentality changed, though, when they explained that when saying "disabled person," it's as if you're putting the disability before the person, whereas if you say "person with a disability," you're putting the person before the disability.

While I'm still not a fan of political correctness, I'll admit that what I learned that day at the CIL made sense. Since then, I make a point to say "person with a disability" instead of "a disabled person." I was reminded that first and foremost, I am a person created by a loving God who has a unique plan for my life. The disability God allowed in my life was not put there to keep me from living my life, but was put there to help me know how best to live my life and make the most positive impact on those around me.

After leaving the CIL, we drove to our next destination in Berkeley, the Ed Roberts Campus (www.edrobertscampus. org). This location was named after the late Ed Roberts, a leader from the early days of the disability rights movement. Roberts, who was severely disabled, spent his life fighting for the rights of the disabled. What makes the Ed Roberts Campus so unique is that it was built on the principle of universal design, a concept which benefits both persons with and without disabilities. Some examples include a helical ramp which winds upwards to the second floor, wide corridors, automatic doors, and hands free sensors and timers for lighting control, to name just a few. At the time of our visit, the facility was still undergoing construction, but upon its completion, the Ed Roberts Campus would become the home of various organizations in the Bay Area that carry on the legacy of Ed Roberts and continue to provide needed help to the disabled so that they may lead better lives.

After leaving the Ed Roberts Campus and having lunch at a dining facility back on the campus of UC Berkeley, we headed to our last stop of the day, the Bay Area Outreach & Recreation Program, also known as BORP (www.borp.org). This organization provides opportunities for persons with disabilities of all ages to participate in year-round sports and recreational activities. Some of their programs have included such things as wheelchair basketball, adaptive cycling, fitness programs, and much more. BORP helps its participants maintain a better fitness regimen which in turn helps them develop better body images, establish healthier living habits, and gain independence.

During our time at BORP, we were given the opportunity to ride some of their three-wheeled cycles used by persons with disabilities because their design makes it easier to handle for some. A makeshift course had been set up on a nearby street with orange cones put in place to keep us out of surrounding traffic. It looked like fun, so I decided to give it a go.

Soon, one of the BORP workers fitted me with a helmet and made sure I was seated properly. She was a very attractive young lady who complimented me on how nice my Southern accent was. (That last sentence really isn't relevant to this story. I just wanted all the single guys out there to know that the word *y'all*, when used enough times, can actually be considered a turn-on by some ladies in parts of the country who aren't used to hearing that particular word that often.)

At first, as I was learning the basics of the pedals and the brakes, it was a little scary, but I soon got the hang of it. As I maneuvered around the cones, I felt this incredible feeling of excitement and independence. I was reminded why it's important to support organizations like BORP with our time, talents, or material resources, so that others can have the same awesome experiences they otherwise might not have.

After leaving BORP, a group of us decided to do a little sightseeing. We drove to the Golden Gate Bridge, and afterwards, several of us did some shopping in Chinatown where I stocked up on souvenirs I desperately needed at the time that are now sitting in my attic collecting dust. After a late dinner in the restaurant at our hotel, we headed back to our rooms to rest up for our final day in San Francisco.

Unfortunately, I didn't get much rest that night. At 2 a.m., I woke up with a sore throat, the kind that makes the act of swallowing a frightening prospect.

By morning, I felt miserable. I had hoped a hot shower would help, but it didn't. On top of everything, I had forgotten to pack a disposable razor to use that day. I have a heavy beard, and if I go just one day without shaving, I begin to look like I could win first place in a Charles Manson look-alike contest. Regardless, we had an itinerary to keep, so I had to keep popping throat lozenges and try to ignore the fact I looked liked I could have starred in a horror flick called *I Was a Legally Blind Werewolf.*

Everyone met downstairs in front of the hotel, and we drove to a nearby bakery for breakfast. (The food would have tasted much better had it not hurt so much to swallow it.) After breakfast, we drove to the site of the federal building in downtown San Francisco where the 504 Sit-in took place in 1977. I realize many readers may not be familiar with this specific sit in, so I'll share a few basic facts.

For starters, we need to look at the Disability Rights and Independent Living Movement, which was prevalent in the 1960's and 70's. According to the UC Berkeley website in a section devoted to the Disability Rights and Independent Living Movement (http://bancroft.berkeley.edu), this movement was important to help the disabled become more of a part of their communities, as opposed to living separate lives from those communities as a result of discrimination with employment, housing, public accommodations, and so forth.

In an article entitled "Short History of the 504 Sit-in" (www.dredf.org) written by Kitty Cone, who was involved in the movement, in 1973, Section 504 of the Rehabilitation Act was signed into law. Section 504 was a law designed to prevent programs that received federal funding from discriminating against persons with disabilities.

Though the law was passed, however, regulations needed to be issued to define who was a disabled person in order for this law to be effective. Proper use of such regulations could provide a clear interpretation of the legal intent of this law instead of leaving it up to judges who heard cases involving Section 504 to make their own personal interpretations.

Within the first few years of Section 504, no regulations were issued, and this helped lead to the creation of the American Coalition of Citizens with Disabilities (ACCD), who were determined to ensure regulations were established. They called for sit-ins to be staged throughout the country.

In April 5, 1977, a sit-in began at the federal building in San Francisco which lasted four weeks. About two weeks into the sit-in, a contingent group was chosen to travel to Washington D.C. for the purpose of meeting with national leaders.

After the media coverage that soon followed, strong Section 504 regulations were signed, though many argue these regulations weren't enforced like they should have been. Regardless, Section 504 did provide clear federal civil rights protection for the disabled, and also showed the country what those protesting, many of whom were disabled, were capable of achieving. Many argue that without 504, there may never have been an Americans with Disabilities Act.

As we all stood outside the federal building, I was greatly impacted by what I learned about the 504 Sit-in from our guide. I realized just how much people like me who are disabled owe to those who fought for our rights decades earlier. We may never have met them, but we still owe them a debt of gratitude.

After a visit to our last destination of the trip, the LightHouse for the Blind and Visually Impaired (http://lighthouse-sf.org), another great agency in the Bay Area which helps the disabled, my manager, Kim, and I left for the airport for our flight back home.

Flying cross-country while sick (by now my sore throat had turned into an all-out sinus infection) isn't fun, especially when sitting in coach in the center seat. Thankfully, Kim took pity on me and let me have the window seat.

Hours later, I was introduced to the beauty of watching the sun set from thirty thousand feet in the air. It's truly breathtaking and makes you gain a greater appreciation for all the beauty in the world you might not notice under different circumstances.

It's easy to see the beauty in a sunset, but it's not always as easy to see how truly beautiful something is by just looking at it.

The same is true when people see someone with a disability. Many times they find themselves preoccupied by how the person looks in a wheelchair, or walks with a cane, or how they speak, or any of the other negative things people associate with being disabled.

What we all need to focus on, however, are all the positive things about people with disabilities, such as their determination, drive, and all the God-given talents and abilities they possess despite that disability. Once we learn to focus on these things, we stop seeing "the disabled person" and start seeing "the person with the disability."

In summing up my experiences in San Francisco, I can honestly say "Perspectives on Inclusion" helped change my perspectives on inclusion.

Several weeks after returning home from San Francisco, I received a phone call at home from the head of my store's personnel department. She wanted to know if I would be willing to fly to our Home Office and accept an award at a special celebration honoring the twentieth anniversary of the Americans with Disabilities Act. Of course, when someone asks you to fly out of state to accept an award, the polite thing to do is say, "Yes." I, however, believe in being super polite, and what I believe I said at the time was, "YESSSS SSSSS!!!!!!!!!!!!!!!!!!!!!!!!!!!!"

Several days later, I was back at the airport, and thankfully Kim had been invited to accompany me once again, which she kindly accepted. This time we flew out of the airport at Jacksonville, and within an hour or so, we landed in Atlanta.

I quickly learned that I don't like flying into the Atlanta

airport. It's incredibly large with way too many people walking through it in way too many directions. I have no love for this airport, and I don't think it's a sin to say this. The Bible says I need to love my enemies, but it says nothing about loving the Atlanta airport.

Thankfully, Kim was there to keep me from getting lost, because I'm certain had it not been for her, I would still be wandering around that airport to this day trying to find Gate Z.A-457.8.

Once we finally found our gate, I began to relax a little, but then we learned there would be a forty-five minute flight delay. I tried to make the best of the situation by reminding myself that since I was working for the company, I was "on the clock" and getting paid. Flight delays are much more bearable when you're getting paid to wait.

Finally, our flight arrived, and we were mercifully pardoned from our imprisonment in Atlanta. An hour or so later we landed at the airport near Home Office located in the middle of the country.

If only our luggage had been able to join us.

Unfortunately, there had been a mix-up, and our luggage was being held hostage in Atlanta (I know how it felt). Thankfully, Kim and I found a friendly airline representative to help us (yes, they do exist), and we learned our luggage would be arriving later that evening.

Moments later, a representative from Home Office, a woman we met during out trip to San Francisco, met us at the airport to take us to our hotel. When she found out what happened to our luggage, she offered to drive us back to the airport after dinner to pick up our bags. A couple of hours later Kim and I were back at the airport, and we were greeted by our two pieces of luggage, both unharmed and untouched, sitting by their lonesome selves on the conveyer belt. It was a good reminder that God not only looks out for us, but He looks out for our luggage, too.

The following morning, Kim and I arrived at home office for the ADA Celebration. I had never been to Home Office before, and the only description I had of it was from coworkers back home who apparently had never been there, either. I quickly learned that my coworkers were wrong on quite a few details. While we were there, I never saw any barbed wire fences surrounding the property, nor did I ever see any snipers perched on the roof. Also, we didn't use a drawbridge to walk through the front entrance, and I never spotted a single gargoyle.

After receiving "security clearance," we were given a quick tour of the building and taken to lunch in a room off to the side of the auditorium where the celebration would be held. During lunch, I was introduced to more company officials, and even got to have lunch with Robert David Hall, who had retuned to be a featured speaker at the event.

After lunch, it was time to begin the ADA celebration, and we were escorted into the auditorium to the front row. We even had reserved seats with our names on the chairs, spelled correctly and everything.

What can I say? I'm easily impressed.

The ADA event featured a variety of guest speakers, video presentations, and of course, the award presentations. I learned

I was one of three individuals who would be receiving an award, though only two of us were able to attend.

Allow me to share my personal highlights of the celebration: First, there were the video presentations of all the award recipients. In the months leading up to the event, camera crews had come to our individual stores and filmed each of us on the job. At the time, though, I didn't really know how or if the footage would be used.

I remember I was very anxious when I was filmed because I was still working in Electronics at the time, and I wasn't excited about the possibility of a film crew documenting my incompetence.

The film crew was amazing, though. They selected the best footage of me at work, and as I watched the footage, I remember thinking, *Wow, I really give the impression that I'm actually knowledgeable.*

Good editing is truly a God-given gift.

Soon, it was time for presentation of the awards. By this time I learned the other gentleman there that day to receive an award, who was in a wheelchair, played a big role in helping the disabled. In his spare time he fixed old wheelchairs to make them usable again for those who needed them.

When it came time to accept my award, I couldn't help but think about everything this gentleman had done to help others. This made me think about everything I *could* have done to help others but hadn't. I kept asking myself, *Have I done enough?*

I began comparing myself to the other award winner. This man had a disability far worse than mine, and yet, I felt he had done more than I had ever done to help the disabled. And what about all those people back in San Francisco? Despite their disabilities, they staged a successful sit-in to help the disabled. They certainly had done more than me.

The plaque I was awarded that day reads: "In recognition of your service, compassion and advocacy for people with disabilities." Had I really been an advocate for persons with disabilities, though? I mean, I was a good employee. I came to work on time, left on time, and I tried to maintain a positive attitude and help my customers.

I realized while I could have done more to be an advocate for the disabled, that didn't mean I hadn't done anything. By simply doing my job the best I could, I showed that people like me with disabilities deserve the chance to work so they can prove how hard they're willing to work to get the job done. In that sense, I began to realize I had been an advocate for people with disabilities after all.

▮ ▮ ▮

The following month, I had the opportunity to speak at a company-wide manager's meeting in Orlando. As part of the continued celebration of the passing of the ADA, I was given the chance to speak to our store managers from across the country about what's it's like to be a company employee with a disability. My hope was that something I said over the course of the two-day event would help the managers see the need to hire persons with disabilities.

I remember the evening before the first meeting when we had "the rehearsal." I don't think I'm giving away any corporate secrets here when I say that people who speak at these types of events need to know what they will be speaking about ahead of time. By the time the rehearsal had ended, it was clear I needed to figure out what I was going to say myself; otherwise I feared getting fired by hundreds of managers all at the same time.

I remember lying in bed in my hotel room that evening trying to figure out what I would say on stage in a few hours. Public speaking can be rough to begin with, and with my vision problems, just walking on and off a stage would pose a challenge. I reassured myself that at least if I did end up falling off the stage at least everyone would know I wasn't faking being legally blind. I rehearsed what I would say and got a basic outline together in my mind.

Later that morning, it was time for the first meeting. As I walked onto the stage (and didn't fall off, I might add) I was handed a microphone by one of the company executives.

Now was the moment of truth, and the truth was pretty simple: I had to be myself. Whatever came out of my mouth had to be from the heart. Being well-rehearsed is great, but not if you end up sounding like a computerized robot.

Over the next two days, with every presentation I gave, I changed it around so that every group I spoke heard something a little different. While the words may have been different, however, the message wasn't. I truly believe God had given me this opportunity to reach others with my words. During my last presentation, which was held shortly after seven in the morning (a time of day I'm not accustomed to public speaking, but rather private sleeping), I concluded my talk with the words from my third book, *Confessions of a Professional Gummy Bear*

Giver Outer, which I was in the process of publishing at the time.

I said "… no matter who we are or what we do, when we work with others, we must be willing to work together as a team. This includes letting others that are different from us, including the disabled, be a part of that same team. A person may not always be able to be the 'hands,' 'feet,' or 'eyes' of the team, but if they have the desire to do the best they can and encourage others to do the same, they will quickly become the 'heart' of the team."

Over those two days, I spoke to hundreds of managers from parts of the country I had never been to before and perhaps never will. I could only hope that when it was over, they would take my words home with them.

I don't know what impact I had on those managers. I can't say for sure if any persons with disabilities were hired because of anything I said or did. What I do know is that I spoke the truth, and God willing, I planted a few seeds. It would be up to someone else to make sure those seeds were given the opportunity to grow into something, or in this case, *someone,* fruitful.

▪ ▪ ▪

Not long ago I had an experience at the gas station I feel is worth sharing. I was standing in my office and noticed a minivan pull up to the gas pump closest to my office window. I couldn't help but notice the van looked like it was designed for someone in a wheelchair.

Moments later, an older woman in a wheelchair did emerge from the van and wheeled herself to the gas pump. While I've had customers who were disabled and didn't need my assistance at the pump, I felt this wasn't the case this time, so I walked out to see if she needed any help.

It turns out she did need my help. She handed me her membership and credit cards so I could swipe them in the pump. I then pressed the buttons on the pump that needed pressing. Since she was able to fill up the tank herself, I handed her the nozzle as I selected the grade of fuel she wanted. She began to fill up the tank, and as we talked, I watched her to make sure she was okay.

When she was done, she handed me the nozzle which I put back safely in its proper place. I handed her the receipt, she said thank you, and then she wheeled back into her van and drove off.

To many, this would seem like a pretty mundane experience, but it helped serve as a reminder that every person has things they can do, things they can't do, and things they *could* do if someone would help them.

In this case, the woman in the wheelchair who I'm guessing couldn't walk, or at least had difficulty doing so, could still drive into the gas station. I have the ability to walk, but I can't drive, so therefore I needed someone to drive me to work that day so I could be there to help her.

While she still needed my help to use the gas pump, when it came time to fill up the tank, all I had to do was hand her the nozzle and she took care of the rest.

Isn't this the way God intended life to be? He gives every

person specific talents and abilities, and He wants us to use those talents and abilities to help one another as needed. I know this isn't the way life always works, but it can work this way if we allow God to guide us.

In the months I traveled the country, I spoke to hundreds, perhaps thousands of people. I was given many opportunities to show them what someone with a disability can accomplish. I never could have done any of this, though, had I not had help along the way. From my supportive family and friends along with everyone at my company who helped me, it has truly been a team effort. I'll forever be grateful to have been a part of such a great team.

⛽ ⛽ ⛽

The Road to Humility: Two months after speaking in Orlando, I was given two additional opportunities to travel for my company. Over a two week period I would travel to store locations throughout North Carolina one week and Virginia the following week to speak at in-store disability awareness events. By this time I was working at the gas station and was excited to have this chance to travel because the average gas station attendant only gets so many opportunities for out-of-state speaking engagements.

What was even greater about these trips was that this time I would be traveling by car. There would be no flying whatsoever!

Better yet, no Atlanta airport whatsoever!!!

Sadly, my friend Kim wouldn't be accompanying me on this round of trips, but I was grateful to her for being willing to travel with me to San Francisco, Home Office, and even Orlando as well. She had a great attitude, and I know she had as much fun as I did. Why wouldn't she? She was the recipient of three trips in a row where someone else paid for her airfare, meals, and hotel accommodations. There are people who make their living as professional game show contestants who aren't that fortunate.

This time I would be traveling with our Market Manager in North Carolina, and the following week I would travel with our Market H.R. Manager in Virginia. They would be doing the driving since I can't drive myself, which gave me the chance to spend my time reading car magazines or napping, activities that are frowned upon while in the driver's seat.

There are a lot of things I like about traveling on the open road, especially on a business trip. Just as I had been getting paid to fly for the company, now I was getting paid to ride for the company. The longer the trip, the more my next paycheck would be. This was the only time in my life where I fervently prayed to get stuck in the middle a traffic jam or massive roadwork on the interstate.

While neither of these scenarios occurred, while in Virginia, my H.R. manager and I were pulled over for speeding. Like any normal human being, he tried to keep the police officer from writing him a ticket, but the officer wouldn't back down. On a great note, though, I was still getting paid for every second we were stopped on the side of the road. To earn a little more money, I considered having a little fun at the H.R. manager's expense and saying to the policeman, "You're not going to look in the trunk, are you, officer?" I chickened out, though, because I was afraid I would end up riding in the trunk for the remainder of the trip.

Another thing I like about traveling on the open road is eating at all the restaurants along the way. There are so many terrifically unhealthy choices out there. When you're flying at thirty thousand feet, there are only so many options available for eating. For me it was like, "Do I eat the stale package of complimentary cookies now, or save it for later for a special treat?"

Of course, the most important part of the trip was speaking at all the different stores and meeting their employees. If truth be told, though, it was a little surreal. Often, when I walked into a store for the first time, I soon noticed it had the same basic floor plan and layout of merchandise as my own store back home. While I eventually got used to this, I never got used to walking into those stores and seeing their employees doing the same jobs as my coworkers back home, and yet I never knew who any of these people were. It was the retail equivalent of being in a parallel universe.

Since we all worked for the same company, though, they began to view me as extended family, sort of like that third cousin twice removed everyone has heard about for years and were now meeting for the first time. It's a relationship built on love, respect, and of course, suspicion.

I remember speaking in one store where I could immediately tell there were morale problems. When I said hello to one employee, she took one look at me in my dress pants and shirt, my sports coat with my name badge, and she had this look of pure fear in her eyes. The first words out of her mouth were, "Are you from Home Office?"

Here's a tip. Never respond to this type of question by saying, "That's for me to know, and you and your soon-to-be fellow former coworkers to find out." (I didn't actually say this; it's just good advice.)

❖ ❖ ❖

Whenever I spoke at a disability awareness event, I always followed the same basic outline. I started talking about my vision issues growing up, how it impacted my job search, finally finding a job at "The Store," and encouraging those I spoke with to reach out and get to know people with disabilities.

The part of my presentation I always enjoyed the most was at the conclusion when I passed out copies of drawings I've done for friends over the years. I draw a pretty good landscape scene, and since I'm nearsighted, it helps me to better see the small details on the objects I draw. I usually don't draw people, though, because I can never seem to get their facial features quite right. They always turn out looking like a Hollywood celebrity shortly before their sixteenth stint in Rehab. I also passed out copies of my earlier books to show everyone, too. During the time I was traveling, I was only weeks away from having my latest book for sale on the shelves of around a dozen of our stores in North Carolina. Whenever people heard me speak about being disabled, I could tell many times at first they felt sorry for me, but after they heard me speak, and once they saw my drawings and books, they were often amazed at what I could do despite being disabled. And, as it often goes, in time my ego started to get the best of me.

Wherever I spoke, I was always received very well, whether it was in Raleigh, Winston-Salem, Greensboro, Durham, Chesapeake, Richmond, Charlottesville, or any other location I spoke at.

And then came Roanoke.

Now, I'm not putting down all the good people of Roanoke, Virginia. I met some great, kind, and downright friendly folks while I was there. The problem was that few, if any, of them attended my presentation.

Here's how I remember my day in Roanoke. My presentation that day was held in the back of the store near the receiving docks. Someone had been kind enough beforehand to set out folding chairs so everyone could sit and even provided cookies for all of us. When I saw this spread and everything that had been done to prepare for my arrival, my ego was working in Hyper Male Ego Overdrive.

It turns out those cookies lulled me into a false sense of security.

This is the part of the story where it gets really painful. I began my presentation like I always did, and talked about how I was born visually impaired. I gave specifics of my condition, called Congenital Optic Atrophy, where the optic nerves in my eyes never fully developed, along with Nystagmus, which makes it difficult for me to focus on objects for long periods of time because my eyes move from side to side rapidly and constantly.

Whenever I talked about my eye conditions, to help put in context, I always told this little joke I made up about me being on a date at a restaurant. (The fact I'm out on a date makes it easy to tell it's made up.)

Anyway, the joke goes on with me saying that I'm looking at my date, and suddenly, an attractive waitress walks by, and my eyes go off my date and I begin looking at the waitress. My date gets mad and says, "Were you looking at that waitress?" and I say, "I was looking at her, but it's beyond my control." Any time previously when I told this joke, I always got a big laugh, and most audiences seemed to become more comfortable around me. When I told this joke in Roanoke, however, I began to believe laughing may have been outlawed within the city limits.

I tried to shake it off and keep going. When I came to a point in my presentation that had gotten laughter or applause anywhere else, in Roanoke I got silence. I couldn't even hear crickets in the background. If there were crickets there, they didn't make any noise.

(Welcome to Roanoke, Virginia: Home of the Silent Crickets.)

I was determined to make it through the presentation. After a while, it didn't really matter what I said, though, because most everyone there who was still conscious just stared at me.

The whole experience was pretty unnerving. They looked at me like I had corn stuck in my teeth. No, I take that back. Really, they looked at me like I had the farmer who grew the corn stuck in my teeth.

Finally I decided to end the presentation, and by "end," I mean put it out of its misery. At the conclusion I thought about saying, "If my being here today has blessed your life in any way, stomp your foot once on the floor for 'yes' and twice for 'no.' All the 'no' people, just follow my lead."

My time in Roanoke had truly been the low point of my

whole trip. I could tell the store manager felt sorry for me. He tried to cheer me up by offering to buy me some bottled water from the store's cafe. At this point he could have offered to buy me a water tower, and it wouldn't have helped.

Looking back, I think the people at my presentation were the "problem employees," and hearing me talk was a form of disciplinary action. Afterwards, I thought I overheard one of them say to their supervisor, "I promise I won't be late for work ever again. Please don't bring that speaker back."

⛽ ⛽ ⛽

Over the years, I've thought a lot about that day in Roanoke. At no time since have I been invited back to speak there. Frankly, I can think of far more pleasant trips to take, like flying out of Atlanta to visit the Allegedly-Haunted Bunk Bed Hall of Fame.

Life is weird. It seems like the experiences we try the hardest to forget often provide the lessons we should try the hardest to remember.

Recently I read the following saying: "The act of imposing humility upon another person is called 'humiliation.'" I didn't steal these words from a fortune cookie; I stole them directly from Wikipedia, so you know they must be true.

I am firmly convinced God has a sense of humor. He allowed me to be put in a situation where I thought I was there to show others how great I was, but I was quickly brought back down to Earth by a group of people who realized I wasn't any better than anybody else. In this case, there couldn't be humility until

119

there was first humiliation. This was a lesson I didn't want to learn, but I'm grateful I learned it anyway.

If I ever go back to Roanoke to speak at that store, though, I think next time I will tell them I'm from Home Office, and see if that makes any difference. It's a known fact in the business world that if you want others to laugh at your jokes, sometimes they must first fear for their jobs.

❦ ❦ ❦

My Commemorative Pins Await Me in Heaven: There are many creative ways a company can show its employees how much they are valued. In some companies, an employee might earn a large cash bonus or perhaps even a trip to the Caribbean for their hard work.

In my company, we receive commemorative pins.

I'm not putting my company down for giving away commemorative pins, because the ones I've earned over the years mean a lot to me, though some pins do mean more to me than others.

For example, at "The Store," every year an employee goes without having an accident on company property they are awarded an "Accident Free" pin. If they go one year without an accident, they receive one that reads "ONE YEAR ACCIDENT FREE." For two years, it's "TWO YEARS ACCIDENT FREE," and so on.

If the company wants to give out these pins, that's fine, but to me, being awarded such pins mean I've just fulfilled the least of my obligations. Besides, the way some customers treat me and my coworkers, if they see one of us wearing a pin that reads "TWO YEARS ACCIDENT FREE," they act like that's how long we've been housebroken.

Some commemorative pins are special, though, such as the one I earned for winning Employee of the Month. I had always wanted to win Employee of the Month, so one month a couple of years back I decided to campaign for it.

Anyone who wins Employee of the Month at "The Store" wins a small cash prize, but what I really wanted to win was the personal parking space that the Employee of the Month also wins for their month. I wasn't going to let the fact I can't drive a car or even own one keep me from doing all that I could to win my own parking space. In my mind, I equated that parking space with being successful. If I won it, and God forbid I died during the month it was rightfully mine, I planned to be buried under the parking space, even though the next month when someone else won it, I knew I'd probably be dug up and moved.

I launched my official campaign for Employee of the Month on the promise that if I won, I would donate the cash prize to a particular children's charity my company proudly supports.

This campaign promise must have put me over the top, because weeks later it was announced I had won Employee of the Month with the most votes. (I also don't believe anyone else was running that month, and that helped, too.)

A few days later, I made good on my promise and donated the cash prize to its rightful charity, and I was also the proud recipient of my own personal parking space, even though I couldn't use it, but it was my parking space *not* to use at my discretion. Plus, for the first time in my working life I now knew the joy of coming into work and saying, "Which one of you jerks parked in my space?!"

In addition to the commemorative pins, "The Store" has also given out pins for more generic reasons, but still important ones, like being a good leader or having a positive attitude. If you've ever worked in retail, though, you know it can be harder to earn these types of pins than it would be win an Employee of the Month pin.

Through the years, my coworkers and I have had many great brainstorming sessions in our break room about what our company pins would read if we had our say. The following suggestions are my personal favorites:

"Innocent Until Proven Guilty."

"The Management Absolved Me from All Wrongdoing."

"While 'On the Clock,' I Can't Be Held Personally Liable for My Actions." (I don't know if that's really true, but I'd sure like to believe it is.)

"I Survived Roanoke." (A personal favorite)

"If You Can Read the Words on This Pin, You're too Close." (I stole this idea from a bumper sticker, but I don't like being around close talkers so it still works in this case.)

"I Passed the Drug Test with Flying Colors."

And my personal favorite:

"I Donated an Extra Kidney to My Boss and All I Got was This Lousy Pin." (In this case, at least throw in a lousy t-shirt to go with the lousy pin.)

While some employees don't really care about being

awarded any special pins, others take a lot of pride in those pins and proudly wear them. If these people aren't careful, though, wearing the pins can go to their heads. They may have first worn them to show others how great they think the company they work for is, but if they aren't careful, they may end up wearing the pins to show others how great they think they are instead.

While it's certainly great to be rewarded for hard work and going the extra mile, shouldn't the feeling of knowing you worked hard and went that extra mile be reward enough?

Allow me to share one of my favorite experiences. A couple summers ago I was working a shift at the gas station. It was July, and the temperature outside was nearing one hundred degrees (prior to the heat index). It was the kind of day I tried to stay in my office with the A/C on full blast and cold bottled water in my hand.

On this particular day, however, I wasn't that fortunate. Near the beginning of my shift, an elderly woman drove into the station in a pickup truck. She approached me, and I could tell right away she was upset. She was very busy that day, and apparently had borrowed the truck from someone who didn't bother to tell her it was low on fuel. Even worse, she had forgotten to bring her purse with her that held her membership and credit cards, so she couldn't use the pumps.

Needless to say, she was frantic. She was miles away from home, very little gas in the tank, and she thought she was going to be stranded.

By this point I was frantic myself, and being outside in the raging heat wasn't helping. I knew I could swipe one of the generic membership cards we keep at the station for such emergencies for her, so that wasn't a problem, but she still had no way to pay for her gas.

I hurried into my office to call inside the store for help. I talked to a manager and I suggested I buy a gift card for her to use with money I had in my wallet and afterwards the store could reimburse me. They told me they'd call me right back. While waiting for the phone call, I walked out to the woman to make sure she was doing okay. By now she was really upset. She kept putting herself down and calling herself stupid for forgetting her purse. I assured her I didn't think she was stupid at all. She just made a mistake. Women forget their purses. Men forget their wallets. It happens. That's life.

Finally they called me back from inside, and I learned that instead of me buying a gift card, it was decided by the powers that be in the store that they would give the woman a gift card with enough money on it so she could fill her tank. It was teamwork at its best, and I don't think I've ever been prouder to work for my company than I was on that day.

A few minutes later, a woman from Customer Service walked out with the gift card for the woman to use. I swiped my member's card, then the gift card was swiped, and in a matter of seconds, the woman was able to fill up her tank.

I don't think I've ever seen anyone more relieved than this woman on this day. She was grateful for what I had done for her, and I'll admit I felt pretty good about myself, too.

She tried to pay me with some pocket change she had, but I declined her offer. She then asked my name, and I gladly told her. She also asked me if she should tell the store manager about what I had done for her.

I had to think about her offer for a moment. If I said yes, it could have been great for me. I might have been publicly acknowledged for helping her, and maybe even receive a special pin for going the extra mile.

Instead, I insisted she didn't say anything. While it would have been great to be recognized for what I did, I knew just having the opportunity to help this person was reward enough. The feeling I got that day was far greater than any pin I could have been awarded.

A few days later, I came to work and discovered a card addressed to me on my desk. It was a thank-you card from this same elderly woman I helped days earlier. While I don't accept gifts, I do make exceptions for thank-you cards every time. While I left out a few words and don't reveal the name of my company, the card basically reads as follows:

> "Dear Bryon, (Okay, she got my name wrong, but it's the thought that counts, and honestly, in my line of work it's nice to have an alias.)
>
> For all you did to make it possible for me to return to my … house and retrieve my purse so I could continue to do my daily … chores. You saved the day!!!! (Apparently it was a four-exclamation-point day that I saved. I was proud.)
>
> God bless you and ('The Store') family for your trust and faith in me. That is why I shop at ('The Store')!! Because of people & employees like YOU!!

Again, Bless you for being you!!!!"

Her words were ten times greater than any special pin.

🔋 🔋 🔋

Matthew 6:19-21 (NIV) reads: "Do not store up for yourselves treasures on earth, where moth and rust destroy, and where thieves break in and steal. But store up for yourselves treasures in heaven, where moth and rust do not destroy, and where thieves do not break in and steal. For where your treasure is, there your heart will be also."

Earthly rewards like plaques, ribbons, trophies, and even commemorative pins are great, but when you leave this world, you can't take any of these treasures with you. The treasures that truly matter are the ones that last for eternity, and the decisions we make on this Earth will determine what, if any, eternal treasures we will be given.

Being awarded a pin from your boss that reads "Well Done" is great, but being awarded a pin from the Lord Himself that reads "Well Done" is what truly matters.

🔋 🔋 🔋

Wrong Direction, Right Decision? Every day, our lives our filled with choices. From the moment we wake up until the moment we go to sleep, we make countless decisions. "Should I get out of bed or sleep in?" "Should I wear the blue shirt with the tan pants or the white shirt with the black pants?" "Should I have cereal or waffles for breakfast?" "Should I have cereal AND waffles?" "Should I skip the cereal and waffles altogether and have a stack of pancakes?" (In hindsight, perhaps I shouldn't be writing this so close to breakfast.)

As the day drags on, we find ourselves with more choices. "Should I get to work on time or come in late and make an excuse to my boss?" "Should I finish my assignments today or wait until tomorrow?" "For lunch, should I get takeout from Burger King or have a sit down meal at Cracker Barrel?" (Cracker Barrel has great pancakes, by the way, in case you're interested.)

As the day draws closer to an end, yet more choices are made. "Should I leave work on time or sneak away early?" "Should I wait for the traffic light to turn green or run it now and hope there aren't any police around?" "Should I go straight home or go back to Cracker Barrel for another round of pancakes?" (As everyone knows, pancakes are the tastiest after the sun goes down.)

The average person faces a variety of choices every day, and the decisions we make not only affect us, but can also affect those around us, which leads us to our next story.

I was working the closing shift at the gas station. It had been a quiet evening and, at the time, there was only one customer at the pumps. Since he didn't need my assistance, I was in my office giving the impression I was diligently working as I stood under the surveillance camera. (Between the clipboard and the binder I mentioned earlier, I have the ability of giving the impression I'm diligently working down to an art form.)

Moments later, an older car drove into the station and parked on the opposite side of the pump the customer was using. I noticed the driver had come in from the wrong direction, so I decided to do some actual diligent work and politely inform the motorist to move their vehicle. As I walked out of the office, however, I noticed the driver of the wrong-way vehicle, a woman, wasn't getting out to pump gas on her side of the pump. Instead, she remained in her vehicle as she spoke to the man at the pump. It looked like they knew one another and were just talking, so I decided to let it go and not say anything.

A minute or so later, I walked out of my office and saw the lady still talking to the customer. As I got closer, I could begin to hear what they were talking about. Apparently, the woman in the car didn't know the customer at all and had approached him in the hopes he could help her in some way.

From what I saw, it appeared the customer had refused to help her, and she drove off. By this time, though, I was close enough that she saw me, and within a matter of seconds, she stopped her car right where I was standing. My first reaction at the time was to say, "Ma'am, can I help you?" She then asked me if I had two dollars she could have.

I was shocked that somebody I didn't know had approached me and asked for money. As I looked at her, though, something in my heart told me she did need help. I took my wallet out, opened it, and sure enough I did have a couple of dollar bills. I handed her the money, and as she took it, our eyes met. She said, "God bless you." I told her she was welcome, and she drove off.

Whenever I look back on this experience, I ask myself the same question over and over: *Did I do the right thing?* From the standpoint as a store employee, as soon as I learned the woman was trying to solicit money from customers, I should have contacted the store management and let them handle the situation. Had I known sooner, I'm certain I would have done so.

Regardless, I still ask myself *Did I do the right thing?* I mean, what did I know about this woman? I didn't know what she wanted the money for, and still don't to this day. It all happened so fast that I didn't think to ask her why she needed the money. Even if I had, she could have just told me what she thought I wanted to hear so I would give her the money.

Was she going to use the money to buy drugs or alcohol because she was an addict? I don't know. Was she going to use the money to get a cheap meal somewhere because she was hungry and just didn't have the money to get something to eat? Again, I don't know. All I know is a person asked me for help, I had the resources to help, and I chose to do so. I treated her the same way I would want to be treated if I asked for help. Simply put, I followed the Golden Rule.

🔹 🔹 🔹

This encounter with the woman at the gas station always makes me think back to an earlier experience I had during my trip to California. San Francisco, like many urban areas, has a large homeless population. Of course, there are homeless individuals in smaller communities, too, but in larger cities it seems like you notice them more. As I traveled throughout the city, I saw numerous people sleeping on the street, holding up cardboard signs asking for assistance, and so on.

One image stands out in my mind, though. Our group had just finished having dinner at Fisherman's Wharf on our first evening in the city. As we were driving to our hotel, we rode through a large lighted tunnel which had a walkway on the side for pedestrians. While in the tunnel, I noticed a person dressed in worn black clothes walking slowly while pushing a shopping cart full of what appeared to be blankets and other paraphernalia. I couldn't tell you the person's age, race, or even gender, but that image has stuck in my mind for years. While I don't know if this person was homeless, from what little I saw, there was a good possibility they were. If this was the case, I wondered if they had ever tried to seek help, and if so, were the people they sought out willing to help?

I wasn't in a position that evening to help that lone figure in black in the tunnel, but that night at the gas station, I realized this woman who asked me for two dollars had become my own figure in black.

🝔 🝔 🝔

With each passing day as I see more and more images on television, the newspaper, the internet, and in my own personal life of people suffering from one tragedy after another, I find myself asking the question "Why does God allow bad things to happen?"

As a Christian who has been involved in the church for as many years as I have, you would think I would be an expert on this sort of thing, but I'm not. In fact, I find myself still praying to God and simply asking "Why?"

It's taken me a long time, but here's what I've come to believe. I believe God loves us and wants the best for us. After all, He gave us His only Son, Jesus Christ, to provide for our salvation. Because He loves us so much, though, He also gives us free will and allows us to make our own choices. He doesn't force us to do anything we don't want to do. When we make the wrong choices, however, sometimes there are very bad outcomes, and it can cost us greatly. Of course, there are many other people who make good choices and they still end up suffering, and it doesn't make sense.

I believe, though, we live in a world filled with deep spiritual darkness and sin (yes, I realize the word *sin* hasn't been fashionable for a few decades now, but I'm going to use it anyway.) We suffer as a result of sin in our lives, and we can also suffer from the sins of those around us. Sometimes the outcome is simply beyond our control.

I believe God put the woman who wanted the two dollars into my life to remind me I've been blessed with so much, and I need to be willing to share a portion of what I have to help others. In fact we all should strive to do this.

I'm not implying we should give all of our hard earned money away to every stranger on the street who asks for a handout. We need to use wisdom and discernment in how we give so that we can help those who *really* need help and not just those who say they need it. By helping those God has put into our lives, however, we learn the importance of showing kindness, mercy, and love to others, which in turn, makes us the kind of people God wants us to be. It's also possible the people we help today may end up being some of the same ones who help us when we need a little help in the future. After all, everybody needs help at some point along the way.

So, when it comes to helping others, do we turn our backs or open our hearts? The choice is ours.

▪ ▪ ▪

And Now, As Promised, the Minivan or Two: One of the things I like best about being a gas station attendant is getting to see all the different makes and models of automobiles that come to the gas station each day. Ever since I was a kid, I've had a love for cars. Like many little boys, if it had four wheels on it, I was immediately hooked. To this day, I still collect toy cars, and as of now, I have a collection of hundreds of Hot Wheels and Matchbox cars. My personal car collection is probably what Jay Leno's car collection would be like if he ended up earning the salary of a gas station attendant as opposed to ending up on television.

It's always fun whenever someone drives into the gas station in a brand new car model I haven't seen in person before that day. Car designs over the last few years have been incredible, but it seems to me these days all new cars look alike. When I was a kid, you could tell right away if you were looking at a Ford or a Chevy or whatever, but it's not that easy anymore. Sometimes when I ask a customer if they're driving a certain model of car, they even get offended. Apparently mistaking an Acura for a Kia is the unpardonable sin in the automotive world.

The cars I love seeing the most at work are the classic cars from days gone by. Nothing brightens my day more than seeing a '55 Chevy or a '63 Pontiac or a '48 Plymouth pull up to a gas pump. These are true classics. Sadly, now that I'm in my thirties, the cars that were new during my childhood are also considered classics, too. (Note: A person is also "not as young as they used to be" when cars made *after* their birth are considered classics.)

I've noticed something interesting about classic car owners. They usually fall into two distinct groups. With some classic car owners, they love if it you just walk up to them and start talking to them about their cars. Sometimes they even let you look under the hood, or take pictures of the car, or even sit in the car. Other classic car owners, however, feel that if you even breathe on their car, it's grounds for justifiable homicide.

I've noticed it's not just classic cars that are admired by customers at the gas station, though. Lots of different cars attract attention. I've lost track of the number of times one customer will walk up to another customer and compliment them on their new pickup truck with the fancy paint job or their late model sports car with the sporty rims or whatever catches their eye. After a while, I start to notice which types of cars get the most attention, and which ones never seem to get any attention at all.

I'm, of course, talking about minivans. Minivans are great vehicles. They're good on gas, they're comfortable to ride in on long trips, and they have lots of room, which is why many families rely on the minivan.

Still, the average minivan is often ignored. You see a minivan in a parking space, and you walk past it and never give it a second thought. You walk past a Corvette or a Camaro, however, and you're still drooling over it hours later.

A while back, I tried a little experiment at work. Whenever a customer drove into the gas station in a minivan, I made a point to walk over to them and compliment them on how great I thought their minivan was. Once the initial shock wore off, most people were genuinely flattered. Judging from some of their reactions, I believe I was actually the first person to ever compliment them on their minivan.

I don't believe minivans get the respect they deserve. The average minivan isn't what you could call flashy, and it often just blends into the background, despite usually being reliable and having the qualifications needed to get the job done. Instead, a lot of people tend to notice the sportier cars, simply because they're faster and look nicer.

I love sports cars, too, but they do have drawbacks. They're often small, so they don't have much room to carry many people or their belongings. They can often be high maintenance, and if something goes wrong, it can cost a lot more to fix. A lot of sports cars also attract attention from people you really don't want your car noticed by, like car thieves or the police when you're late for work and you're doing seventy miles per hour in a school zone, which, as you well know, you should never do. The only people that should be allowed to do this are authorized emergency personnel, like police, paramedics, and teachers.

I've noticed people are often treated like minivans and sports cars. Many times people prefer to be around "the sports cars" because they're prettier, more popular, and stylish. The "minivans" often get ignored and pushed to the side because they aren't as popular or well-liked, even though they can do so many things the "sports cars" can't do well at all.

Cars come in all shapes and sizes, and so do the people who drive them. People, like cars, can be small or large, plain or flashy, and some are in great shape, whereas in others, the dents and dings in life are easily seen.

God, however, made all of us a certain way for a certain reason, and He loves both the "minivans" and the "sports cars" equally. Even better, while the value of most cars depreciates over time, God's "cars" always hold their value.

Remember, we're all here together in this "Parking Lot of Life," and whether you're a "minivan" or a "sports car," sooner or later, there's going to be a runaway shopping cart headed straight for your driver's side door. If God is your driver, though, that extra dent or ding won't make Him love you any less, and you can rest easy knowing He'll *never* trade you in for another model.

▪ ▪ ▪

As you read about the milestones, memories, and even the minivans in my life, it's easy to see how the last five years of my career have given me a lot to think about, and I hope what you've just read has given you a lot to think about, too.

For a part-time hourly wage worker I've had some great opportunities, and I think I have made pretty good use of the time I've been given. I do regret, however, not using some of that time to take some art lessons, because had I done so, it might have changed the outcome of our next and final chapter.

Chapter 4

Drawing Conclusions

Just like my love for cars, since I was a kid, I've also had a love for art. Since childhood, I've spent many hours with a sketchpad and pencil in my hand drawing away, creating whole new worlds on paper. I learned early on I wasn't a natural-born athlete, so my parents knew right away it would be safer for everyone involved to keep me stocked up on art supplies to continue to help me create those whole new worlds. Had they given me a football or baseball, I would have easily destroyed our existing world.

When I was a boy, I often combined my love for cars and art by drawing major car wrecks. The best way to describe my artwork in what I call "The Demolition Derby Series" is to say it looked like the aftermath of a Ford full of radical Lutherans on their way to blowing up a gas station colliding with Lady Gaga driving a Prius with a gun rack on top. Thankfully as I grew older, I got out of my car crashing phase and started drawing considerably more eye pleasing landscape scenes, which I wrote about briefly in the last chapter.

In addition to my love for art, I've also had a long-time love of art programs on television. I'm a pretty anxiety-prone person to begin with, and I've found that watching an art program is far more cost effective than going to the doctor and getting put on blood pressure medication. It always amazes me when I watch any art program where in just thirty minutes, an artist can take a blank canvas, and by the time the closing credits are rolling on the screen they have created a masterpiece.

Of all the television artists I watch, I'd have to say Bob Ross has always been my favorite. His voice is always so calming, and he draws great nature scenes. When I was flying back from San Francisco years ago, watching that beautiful sunset from thirty thousand feet with the clouds underneath, I remember thinking this looks like something Bob Ross would have drawn just before he would draw a completely unnecessary large "Happy Tree" that never should have been in the scene to begin with.

Actually looking back, the fear of Bob Ross drawing "Happy Trees" always did make my blood pressure rise a bit. Maybe that's good, though, because for most of the program, I was so relaxed I may actually have been clinically dead.

⛽ ⛽ ⛽

Two years ago I decided to enter a couple art competitions and see what would happen. The first competition I entered was a local county-wide competition where I entered a black and white sketch I drew of an historic North Carolina home surrounded by trees. I was very proud of this drawing, and I felt confident I would win. Well, I learned confidence doesn't go as far as it used to because I lost.

About a month later, I entered another art competition, but this time it was a bigger contest being held by "The Store." It was a company-wide art contest where the guidelines were to create artwork that showed images of our company's core values, such as striving for excellence in service to our customers and respect for one another.

For the next three weeks, I labored over what I knew in my heart would be an award winning drawing. The closer I got to finishing, the better I thought my chances were of winning. By the time I sent off my entry, I was dealing with yet another visit from the Dreaded Male Ego.

Fortunately, the Dreaded Male Ego didn't stay very long, because once again, I didn't win the contest. I'm not sure, but I think the judges may have all come from Roanoke and were already familiar with my work. On a good note, though, since I've had my art rejected both locally and nationally, I think that means I can now call myself a true artist.

I hated to see my drawing go to waste, so out of the kindness of my store management's heart, they accepted a copy of my entry, which to this day still hangs on the wall of our store training room.

Many times during my lunch break I eat alone in the training room. I know it's antisocial, but I like the peace and quiet in there that I can never seem to get in the employee break room. The sound of a dozen workers texting at once is rather overwhelming.

As I sit in the training room eating my peanut butter and jelly sandwich and apple slices, I often look up at that copy of my drawing. In many ways it's proven to be quite inspirational, at least for me.

The drawing is divided into four sections with each section showing a different image of me doing jobs I've performed over the years at "The Store." In one image, I drew myself working in Electronics explaining the difference in two laptop computers to a customer. If only I knew how to operate a computer as well as I can draw one, perhaps I would have lasted longer in that department.

In another panel I drew myself helping another customer in the office supply aisle, which was also part of the Electronics Department when I worked there. Thankfully, I have a much better grasp of office supplies. I know how a pencil works, and writing with pencils is much easier than writing with computers. Pencils are less complicated. If you get a virus while writing on your computer, you're in a lot of trouble. If you get a virus while writing with a pencil, however, you just spray it down with Lysol and resume writing.

In another panel I drew myself and a random coworker helping load a mattress into a cart for a customer. Mattresses were also part of the Electronics department for some reason. I learned early on always to ask for help in loading any mattress larger than a Twin size. If I tried lifting a King or Queen size mattress by myself, the end result would be me drawing myself being loaded in the back of an ambulance in a picture for a company-wide safety poster contest.

In the final panel (my personal favorite), I drew myself working at the gas station. I'm shown helping a woman at a gas pump. If I do say so myself, I look pretty great in the drawing. This is due partly to the fact I drew myself ten pounds lighter than I am. Plus, I made sure to draw myself wearing my bright orange cap, so you can't see my hair loss. Also I look taller than normal because I accidentally drew my neck longer than it is.

Despite all those great images of me at work (though the one of me at the gas station could have been easily confused for a giraffe wearing a reflective vest), I have to resign myself to the fact that my artwork will probably never be seen by thousands of people nationwide, but it has been seen by my coworkers, and in the end, they mean far more to me than those thousands of people I'll never meet ever will.

As I come to the conclusion of this book, I find myself starting to feel at the proverbial loss for words. Just as an earlier chapter title implied, I felt pumped at the start and now I'm coasting on fumes. If this book was a car, I would feel like I'm staring at a big "E" on the fuel gauge and praying I make it to the gas station in time to fill up before the pumps shut off for the night.

I think the best way for me to conclude is by asking everyone reading this book the following question: After reading this book, has your perception of gas station attendants changed for the better?

If the answer is no, then I'm sorry you feel this way, but if you bought this book from me, you're still not getting a refund. If your perception of gas station attendants has changed for the better, however, then I can now breathe a sigh of relief knowing this little writing project I began months ago was well worth the effort.

To sum it all up, in the eyes of the world, a gas station attendant may never be looked upon with great esteem, but in the eyes of the God who made this world, that same gas station attendant is held in high regard. If God holds us in high regard despite the jobs we each do, then we should also hold one another in high regard despite the jobs we each do because all our jobs are important in their own unique ways.

To everyone out there like me who finds themselves in a job they never set out in life to do but still do it anyway, don't give up. Find the good in what you do. Find the humor in what you do. Most importantly, look to God for strength and guidance in all you do.

To all the wonderful customers out there who keep us gas station attendants gainfully employed, thanks for giving us the opportunity to be a part of your lives. To the customers I serve personally, please know as you drive into the gas station, I look forward to making sure you get the service you deserve, even if you drive in carrying a truckload of allegedly haunted bunk beds that just happened to come out of a small town in Wisconsin. If this scenario happens, I'll likely be running away from the gas station. As I'm running across the parking lot, however, I'll still try to find a cart guy to come over to help you. I'm sure he'll be more than happy to oblige.